A. F. Pollard

Political Pamphlets

A. F. Pollard

Political Pamphlets

ISBN/EAN: 9783337075095

Printed in Europe, USA, Canada, Australia, Japan

Cover: Foto ©ninafisch / pixelio.de

More available books at **www.hansebooks.com**

POLITICAL PAMPHLETS

SELECTED AND ARRANGED

BY A. F. POLLARD

*WITH AN INTRODUCTION AND
EXPLANATORY NOTES*

LONDON
KEGAN PAUL, TRENCH, TRÜBNER & CO.
1897

PREFATORY NOTE

TO

'THE PAMPHLET LIBRARY'

THE object of *The Pamphlet Library* is to set before readers who are interested in the literary and constitutional history of our country the text of those pamphlets or tractates which, besides possessing the only saving qualities of distinction and style, have also exercised a striking influence upon the current of events. At present four volumes are in contemplation, dealing respectively with pamphlets of political, literary, religious, and dramatic significance, and the editors who have undertaken them have regulated their choice primarily by two considerations. Each pamphlet, it has been held, should have high literary qualities, and should also mark a distinct change or development of taste or standpoint. Unfortunately, the pamphleteer of the seventeenth and eighteenth centuries was not always as brief as he was effective, and the restrictions of space have obliged the omission of some polemical articles which might possibly have been included with advantage. It is hoped, however, that by means of excerpt and footnote no pamphlet of the first importance has been altogether neglected; and the editors of the various volumes explain in their introductions the reason and the limit of their selections. Concerning the value of the Pamphlet and the expediency of its recension, Dr Johnson himself will be found discoursing with pregnancy and wit in Mr Ernest Rhys's Literary Collection, and his strenuous sentences are more than sufficient argument in favour of the present enterprise. For, indeed, Reform is the child of Controversy, and the most effectual arrows in the quiver of Controversy are those of a country's Press. Before the day of the clamouring newspaper, the Pamphlet was the leader of popular taste, so that in a study of these fugitive pieces we may see the features of an Age, as in a glass, may mark its expression, and understand its tendency. As some such footnote to history the following papers have been collected. How far they may prove of value it rests with others to decide.

A. W.

CONTENTS

		PAGE
INTRODUCTION	. . . . .	9
I. SEXBY'S KILLING NO MURDER	. .	33
II. HALIFAX'S ROUGH DRAFT OF A NEW MODEL AT SEA	. . . .	37
III. HALIFAX'S CAUTIONS FOR CHOICE OF MEMBERS OF PARLIAMENT	. .	58
IV. ARBUTHNOT'S ART OF POLITICAL LYING		105
V. STEELE'S CRISIS	. . . . .	124
VI. SWIFT'S THOUGHTS ON THE PRESENT STATE OF AFFAIRS	. . . .	133
VII. BOLINGBROKE'S STATE OF PARTIES AT THE ACCESSION OF GEORGE I.	.	170
VIII. SWIFT'S DRAPIER'S LETTERS NO IV.	.	191
IX. JUNIUS'S LETTER NO I.	. . . .	223
X. JUNIUS'S LETTER TO THE DUKE OF BEDFORD	. . . . .	239
XI. JUNIUS'S LETTER TO THE KING	. .	253
XII. BURKE'S THOUGHTS ON THE CAUSE OF PRESENT DISCONTENTS	. . .	278
XIII. BURKE'S LETTERS ON A REGICIDE PEACE NO III.	. . . . .	340

INTRODUCTION

THE first difficulty that meets the editor of a selection of political pamphlets is the need of arriving at some definition of what a pamphlet, and particularly a political pamphlet, is. The word itself is of some antiquity; it occurs in the *Philobiblon* of Richard of Bury, Bishop of Durham, who died in 1345. But its etymology is involved in obscurity; Myles Davies, who published in 1715 a work called *Icon Libellorum: or, A Critical History of Pamphlets*, gives four different derivations, none of which would satisfy the requirements of modern philology. Indeed, the only thing certain about the word seems to be that it has always been considered equivalent to the Latin 'libellus' and to have meant a 'little book.' As to the contents of the political pamphlet, a definition of their nature must, like most definitions, be approximate rather than exact. It is impossible, for instance, to draw a hard and fast rule between the pamphlet and the essay or treatise on political philosophy. It is of the essence of a political pamphlet that it should have an immediate and specific political purpose; it seeks to influence opinion and win votes in view of a particular question; it appeals to the man in the street rather than to the man in the study, to the many rather than to the few; it requires an extensive and rapid circulation, and hence it must be cheap in price and moderate in bulk. To the treatise on political philosophy, popularity is a matter of comparative indifference; its nature is theoretical rather than practical, and it seeks to influence thought rather than action. Its object is in a sense political: Locke furnished a philosophical basis for the political dogmas of the Whigs, Hobbes and Filmer attempted a similar service for the Tories, but no one would call the *Essay on Toleration, Civil Government*, the *Leviathan* or the *De Patriarcha* a political pamphlet. The distinction is not always so clear; no treatise on political philosophy is richer in that science than Burke's *Reflections on the French Revolution;* no book ever appealed more strongly to the student of politics. Yet it is a political pamphlet; it sought a single definite political object—the overthrow of the French Revolution; and if, incidentally, it lays down profound political maxims, if, by way of illustration, it appeals to the broadest political truths, it proves not that it is not a political pamphlet, but that it is a great one.

Still more blurred and indistinct are the lines which separate the political from the ecclesiastical or religious pamphlet on the one hand and the literary pamphlet on the other. Some of the greatest pamphlets are political in one aspect and literary in another; others are at the same time political and ecclesiastical. Milton's *Areopagitica* deals with a great political question, the freedom of the press. No less political was the question of toleration and the civil status of dissenters, which produced some of the finest pamphlets in the language; such are Defoe's *Shortest way with Dissenters*, Halifax's *Letter to a Dissenter* and *Anatomy of an Equivalent*, and Swift's *Sentiments of a Church of England man*. But it is easy to carry this principle of definition too far; almost every question has a political aspect, and by a little ingenuity the term 'political' can be made to cover every pamphlet in the language. It belongs more properly to those only in which the political is the sole or at least the predominant element.

It will be at once apparent that the existence of the political pamphlet is subject to certain conditions which can only be obtained in certain stages of political, social, and intellectual development. It is essentially a means of popularising political thought and stimulating political action in masses of men, and there is obviously no function for it in a state where political power is engrossed in the hands of one or of the few. Its existence therefore presupposes a certain amount of constitutional freedom. Intellectual progress is no less indispensable; pamphlets could be of little use until a certain proportion of the people were able to read them, and there could be few pamphlets at all before the existence of a printing press. As we have seen the word dates from a time when the only means of popularising a work consisted in making numerous manuscript copies, or in putting the idea in the form of political songs which could easily be remembered. Perhaps no pamphlet ever produced such an effect as John Ball's rhymed couplet—"When Adam delved and Evè span, who was then the gentleman?" and the number of manuscript copies made of Richard Rolle's mystical works would probably be considered a fair circulation for a printed book to-day. Yet such means can scarcely be said to have adequately filled the place of a printing press. Nor was Gutenberg's invention at once followed by a development of political pamphleteering. The dominant interest in the sixteenth century was anything rather than political; and the printing press devoted itself first to the revival of classical learning and then to the religious discussions which followed the Reformation. Pamphlets took a religious, literary, and dramatic form before they entered on the domain of politics; the Marprelate tracts (1588), the *Defence of Poesie* (1581), and Heywood's *Apology for Actors* (1612) are all prior to the publication of any political pamphlet of note. It was not till the popular acquiescence in the strong national government of the Tudors was succeeded by revolt against the feeble dynastic policy of the Stuarts, that interest in politics became dominant in national life. The long contest between king and parliament drew literature into its vortex, and from it emerged the political pamphlet.

The floodgates of political writing were now opened, but the volume of political pamphlets that covered the country was remarkable for quantity rather than quality. During the Civil War, news-sheets like the *Mercurius Politicus, Mercurius Aulicus* and *Mercurius Britannicus* made their appearance; of the number of pamphlets more strictly so-called some idea may be gained by turning over the collection of 'King's Pamphlets' in the British Museum, by a glance through the ten volumes of selections called the 'Somers Tracts' and the similar 'Harleian Miscellany,' or even by consulting Maseres' 'Select Tracts relating to the Civil War.' Prynne alone published two hundred books and pamphlets, and a less known predecessor, Thomas Scot, was fairly prolific; few of his pamphlets can be certainly traced to him, but those few number between forty and fifty. Most of these pamphlets are of a very ephemeral character and there are few that do not merit the oblivion that has enveloped them. One or two like Prynne's *Canterburies Doome*, Heylyn's *Cyprianus Anglicus*, Vicars's *Burning Bush* and *God's Ark*, and Bishop Gauden's '$E\iota\kappa\omega\nu\ \beta\alpha\sigma\iota\lambda\iota\kappa\grave{\eta}$, which passed through forty-seven editions, have a permanent historical interest, but it is not due to their literary value. Others, like the tracts of Hugh Peters, derive importance from the political part played by their authors. But the majority of writers are, like Tobie Venner and Marchamont Nedham, as obscure as their works, though the latter was in 1649 paid £50 by the Council of State for his *Case of the Commonwealth State*. Even Andrew Marvell's pamphlets are forgotten, though in his own age his reputation rested mainly on them, and Swift thought they entitled him to be considered a great genius. One name indeed, that of John Milton, stands out from the herd of pamphleteers, and some of his pamphlets have become permanent additions to English literature. There is but one other production of the commonwealth, *Killing No Murder*, that has escaped oblivion.

The Restoration and consequent suppression of the freedom of the press caused a temporary lull in political writing, but it was only the prelude to the golden age of pamphleteering which extended from the Revolution to the close of the eighteenth century. The final transference of political power to the House of Commons, and through it to the constituencies, corrupt and limited though they were, at once put a high value on the political writer, and the rise of the two great parties, Whig and Tory, opened a ready market for his wares. At the same time the lapse of the Licensing Act in 1695 removed the greatest obstacle to the development of pamphleteering. Newspapers like the *London Post*, the *Flying Post*, the *Postboy*, the *Postman*, and a host of others, made their appearance, and side by side with newspapers, political pamphlets grew in importance. Pamphleteers were no longer obscure hacks, ready to sell their pen to the highest bidder, but the foremost statesmen and greatest men of letters in the land. Halifax was followed by Defoe, Swift, Steele, Addison, Arbuthnot, Bolingbroke, and Burke, and they carried on the line of great pamphleteers till pamphleteering was supplanted by other forms of political literature and other methods of political warfare.

It is hard to understand the neglect that has overtaken the literary productions of George Savile, Marquis of Halifax. Ranke calls him 'one of the finest pamphleteers that have ever lived,' and Mackintosh considered his *Letter to a Dissenter* 'the finest specimen of occasional literature extant.' No contemporary writing illustrates better the politics of the time, and few pamphleteers have made keener observations on events passing around them or treated them in so philosophic and scientific a spirit; while his terseness of expression and pointedness of phrase have rarely been excelled. Yet none of his pamphlets seem to have been reprinted in any selection of political tracts, and with the exception of some extracts in Mr Henry Craik's *English Prose Selections* they are inaccessible to the majority of readers. Defoe has met with more worthy recognition, partly because of his eminence in other branches of literature and partly, perhaps, because his *Shortest Way with Dissenters* gained him the distinction of the pillory—a distinction which he converted into a triumph by his *Hymn to the Pillory*. He wrote two hundred and fifty-four works, and his best known political piece is probably his *True-born Englishman*, published in 1701. The other great Whig pamphleteer of Queen Anne's reign was Steele, whose *Crisis* is one of the best known pamphlets in English literature. But the genius of Defoe and Steele paled their ineffectual fires before that of their great antagonist Swift, 'without exception the most effective political writer in England at a time when political writing was of transcendent importance.'[1] Brought up with Whig prepossessions as secretary to Sir William Temple, Swift as a high churchman naturally gravitated towards the Tories during the reign

[1] Lecky, *Hist. of England*, ed. 1892, i. 197.

of Queen Anne. Never did publicist render any party such yeoman service as Swift rendered the Tories, and rarely did anyone meet with such scant rewards. More than anything else, his *Conduct of the Allies* made the peace of Utrecht acceptable to the nation, and if anything could have saved his party from the fifty years' exclusion from office which befell them on the accession of George I., the loyal adoption of the advice he offered in his *Free Thoughts on the Present State of Affairs* would have done it. That advice was rejected; the Whigs monopolised office for half a century, and Swift retired to his deanery in Dublin. There he threw in his lot with his Irish countrymen, and for the first time in history made the cause of Ireland heard even in England in pamphlets of unrivalled sarcasm, wit, and invective.

He left the field in England to Steele, Defoe, Arbuthnot, Addison, and a host of smaller fry like Oldmixon. Many of them are great names in literature, but rather in the character of essayists than of pamphleteers, and they mainly confined their political writing to periodicals like the *Old Whig*, the *Plebeian*, the *Whig Examiner*, and others. With them the generation of Queen Anne's pamphleteers died out. They were succeeded by a group of writers who made the *Craftsman* a terror to Walpole's government, but whose names have been completely overshadowed by that of Bolingbroke, one of the most extraordinary characters in English history. Brilliant as a statesman, he had overturned the ministry of Godolphin and Marlborough when covered with glory, and carried with unexampled address the peace of Utrecht. Then, undermining his rival Harley, he succeeded as first minister of the crown, only to find his position ruined and his schemes wrecked by the death of the queen four days later. Dazzling as an orator, Chatham declared that he would rather recover one of Bolingbroke's orations than the lost books of Livy, or all the gaps in Greek and Roman lore; while as a pamphleteer he has been declared by an eminent living critic[1] to rank only below the three or four highest masters of English prose. Driven into exile on the accession of George I., he took office under the Pretender, but when the rebellion of 1715 failed, he sought to make his peace with the king and secured it by the gift of eleven thousand pounds to George's mistress, the Duchess of Kendal. Returning to England he organised the opposition to

[1] John Morley, *Walpole*, p. 79.

Walpole, and united under his leadership discontented Whigs like Carteret and Pulteney, and honest Tories like Wyndham and Shippen. He made the pages of the *Craftsman* the vehicle for the bitter and effective attacks on Walpole which gradually sapped the minister's power. It was Walpole's cue to represent all Tories as Jacobites; Bolingbroke retorted with his *State of Parties at the Accession of George I.*, in which he strove by skilful misrepresentation to prove that he and his colleagues had never entertained any idea of overturning the Hanoverian succession. But his greatest pamphlet was his *Idea of a Patriot King*, 'a work important equally as a historical document and as a model of style. Chesterfield said that until he read that tract he did not know what the English language was capable of.'[1] His theory was that 'the power and prerogative of the sovereign should be greatly enlarged as the only efficient check upon the corruption of Parliament.'[2] It set up an ideal of a patriot king who would govern independently of all parties and particularly of the Whigs, by means of the ablest ministers, especially Bolingbroke and his friends. It

[1] E. J. Payne, *Select Works of Burke*, vol. i. pp. xvi., xvii.
[2] Lecky, *Hist. of England*, i. 272.

was intended for the instruction of the heir apparent, Frederick Lewis, who was in chronic opposition to his father, and upon it were modelled to some extent the political ideas of George III. To its influence has been traced the loss of the American colonies, and the postponement of Catholic Emancipation; the affiliation is fanciful, but there is no doubt that it tended to enhance George III.'s ideas of the royal prerogative which had no small share in producing the evils of his reign.

What those evils were is vividly pourtrayed in the writings of that pseudonymous entity whom Burke termed the 'prince of pamphleteers.' Whoever the writer may have been who concealed his personality under the name of Junius — and the evidence points decisively in favour of Sir Philip Francis—his literary merits were of the highest order, and his letters have become a classic in English literature. 'No writer ever excelled Junius in condensed and virulent invective, rendered all the more malignant by the studied and controlled deliberation of the language, in envenomed and highly elaborated sarcasm, in clear and vivid statement; in the art of assuming, though an unknown individual, an attitude of great moral and political superiority:

in the art of evading difficulties, insinuating unproved charges, imputing unworthy motives. His letters are perfectly adapted to the purposes for which they were intended. There is nothing in them superfluous or obscure, and nothing that fails to tell. He had to the highest degree the gift of saying things that are remembered, and his epigrams are often barbed with the keenest wit.'[1] They are the work of a man who was a practical politician first and a man of letters afterwards, and his writings are distinguished by a political sagacity and precision of criticism which only a close acquaintance with the practice of politics can give. His motives indeed were not of a high order; personal spite entered largely into them, and many of his letters were written merely to revenge real or fancied wrongs. He hated most of the ministers of his time, and he stopped at nothing in the 'measured malignity of slander' with which he assailed them. Above all he hated the king, and he did not hesitate to insinuate that the king was a coward, not because it was true, but because he knew that the king, who was unmoved by any other charge, would not 'eat meat for a week' after being taunted with lack of courage.

[1] Lecky, *Hist. of England*, iii. 451.

Nor is Junius in any way in advance of his age: keen as his judgment is on many immediate political issues, his letters 'contain no original views, no large generalizations, no proofs of political prescience, no great depth or power of thought;' and the task of elaborating a rival political theory to that of the *Patriot King* was left to his great contemporary Burke.

In the whole scope of political literature there is no writer so often read or so frequently quoted in the present day, and none whose influence has been so deep and lasting, as that of Edmund Burke. It is not merely because of his eloquence or literary style, nor because of the theory of the constitution which he opposed to that of the *Patriot King*, and which was for a century the favourite dogma of conservative statesmen. Nor is it because of the insight with which he treated current political questions; it is neither due to the fact that he urged conciliation with America nor to the fact that he preached war to the death against Revolutionary France. It is because he never touched a subject without adorning it with reflections that go to the root of the principles of government in all ages and all nations. Many of these reflections have become the commonplaces of politics; though as common sense is one of the rarest of qualities, so the commonplaces of politics are often deemed those which may be most safely neglected. *I do not know the method of drawing up an indictment against a whole people* is one of these maxims. *The people have no interest in disorder. When they do wrong, it is their error and not their crime* is another; *whenever a separation is made between liberty and justice neither is in my opinion safe* is a third; and they abound in every pamphlet and every speech from the *Present Discontents* to the *Third Letter on a Regicide Peace*.

In Burke political writing reached its highest development. His *Reflections on the French Revolution* had perhaps a greater immediate effect than any other pamphlet, for except the execution of Louis XVI. nothing did so much to precipitate war between England and France; and it called forth two famous answers—Paine's *Rights of Man* and Mackintosh's *Vindiciae Gallicae*. Erskine's 'Causes and Consequences of the War with France,' which appeared in 1797, and ran through forty-eight editions, was a reply to Burke's *Regicide Peace*. But from this time the art of political pamphleteering progressively declined. Cobbett was a prolific pamphleteer, and Carlyle wrote *Latter Day Pamphlets*, but the vigorous style of the former is little justification for placing him in the same class with the giants of the eighteenth century, and the latter essays scarcely come within the definition of a political pamphlet. Such as they are they are but exceptions to the general decay of pamphleteering. The reasons for which are fairly obvious. The function of the pamphlet as a means of popularising political thought and influencing political opinion is now performed by a multitude of quarterly, monthly, weekly, and daily periodicals. Colonel Sexby might experience some difficulty in persuading an editor to publish his advocacy of political assassination, but a modern Halifax would find a fitting medium for his counsels of political perfection in the pages of the *Spectator*. A latter-day Swift would thunder against the enemies of the church in the columns of the *Times*; a Burke would denounce the infamy of a regicide peace in monthly contributions to the *Nineteenth Century*, while Junius's Letters would be printed amid harmonious surroundings as paragraphs in *Truth*. Through the medium of the daily press the politician from the front benches in parliament, or from the most distant provincial platform, appeals to a wider audience than ever did the pamphleteer. But it would be idle to deny that the presentation of political thought has suffered by the change. It is almost a truism that a speech to read well must be a bad one. The tendency is all towards discouraging set orations, and without elaborate preparation there can be no literary finish. Equally fatal to political writing has been the pace at which men live in the nineteenth century: the quarterly review has been supplanted by the monthly, the monthly by the weekly, and the weekly by the daily press, which, in its turn, is threatened by the evening paper, which publishes its second edition at ten o'clock in the morning and prints another every hour till late in the afternoon. Political discussion is sacrificed to the passion for news; pamphlets are superseded by paragraphs, and head lines do duty for arguments. To parody the words of the greatest and last of the great pamphleteers, the age of the pamphlet is gone, that of the stump-orator and writer of occasional notes has succeeded, and the glory of political writing is extinguished for ever.

In making a selection from the political

literature thus roughly sketched, it is manifest that difficulty arises rather from a wealth than from a dearth of material. The choice must be largely a matter of personal preference, though to others individual taste is apt to appear arbitrary and capricious, and the result a thing of shreds and patches. Nevertheless at least one canon may be laid down without fear of contradiction; no pamphlet has been included that does not possess a permanent literary as well as a permanent historical interest. It is not sufficient that a pamphlet should record historical facts not otherwise known, be they never so important; it must also embody literary qualities of a high order. It would have been easy to select a dozen or a score of tracts from the Somers and Harleian Collections, but the result would not have repaid perusal by any but minute historical students. A more serious difficulty is presented by the mechanical limits of space. Of the greatest political pamphlets not a few would severally occupy volumes far exceeding the present in bulk; such are Swift's *Conduct of the Allies*, Bolingbroke's *Idea of a Patriot King*, Burke's *Reflections on the French Revolution*, and Tom Paine's *Rights of Man*, while Halifax's *Character of a Trimmer*,

Steele's *Crisis* and each of Burke's *Letters on a Regicide Peace* would cover half the present volume; even the latter's *Letter to a Noble Lord* — the most splendid repartee in the language—would fill a quarter of its pages. It thus becomes a question of omitting them altogether and falling back on shorter pamphlets or offering merely extracts; the former alternative has with one or two exceptions, noted below, been adopted.

The pamphlets have generally been arranged in chronological order, and a short note has been prefixed to each detailing the circumstances of its publication. The first is the dedication of Sexby's *Killing No Murder*, the title of which has become a household word. The pamphlet itself is an exercise on the well-worn classical theme of tyrannicide eked out by copious references to Aristotle; its length is considerable, and in literary distinction it falls far below the dedication which is an admirable specimen of ironical writing. Then follow two pamphlets by Halifax, and if the space allotted to them is somewhat disproportionate, the excess may be forgiven in an attempt to redress an unmerited neglect and rescue from obscurity some of the works of a most original and admirable political pamphleteer. The fourth pamphlet here reprinted, *The Art of Political Lying*, is somewhat different in character, being satirical rather than controversial in character. The next three, Steele's *Crisis*, Swift's *Thoughts upon the Present State of Affairs*, and Bolingbroke's *State of Parties at the Accession of George I.*, all deal with the question of the Hanoverian Succession. Only the dedication of Steele's *Crisis* has been reprinted partly because the pamphlet itself is long and partly because it consists largely in a recitation of acts of Parliament, which do not illustrate Steele's style and would probably be found wearisome by the modern reader. The dedication is at once a good example of Steele's literary art and an illustration of his object and point of view. The other two need no apology, as they are among the best of the writings of their respective authors. The last has been printed slightly out of chronological order because of its intimate connection with the other two. Swift's *Fourth Drapier's Letter* is the best of his Irish pamphlets. The three letters of Junius that follow are equally representative. The first opens the series, the second is a typical instance of the methods with which he assailed prominent men of the day, and the third addressed to the king created most excitement of them all. Next comes the first part of Burke's *Thoughts on Present Discontents,* and the volume closes with the peroration of his *Third Letter on a Regicide Peace.*

The decision to print extracts from Burke has not been reached without a struggle and a shudder at the Philistinism of such a proceeding. A competent critic has affirmed that the only specimen of Burke is 'all that he wrote.'[1] But the true lover of art will prefer a torso of Pheidias to all the statues on the Embankment, and no critic of taste will stigmatize the choice of a few fragments from Burke before half a dozen complete tracts of Nedham or Cobbett. Moreover, the design of the present volume is to stimulate, not to surfeit the appetite; to vary the metaphor, it professes merely to offer a few samples with a view to increasing the demand for more. Thanks to the long enjoyment of a free constitution and to a liberty broadening down through centuries from precedent to precedent, the collection of English political pamphlets is unique. No other nation can pretend to rival us in that branch of literature; and the object of this volume will be more than fulfilled if

[1] Hazlitt.

it induces a reader here and there to dip more deeply into this mine of wealth, and study some of those political pamphlets which, written with an immediate and even transitory political purpose, are yet, like the immortal history of Thucydides, κτήματα ἐς ἀεὶ μᾶλλον ἢ ἀγωνίσματα ἐς τὸ παραχρῆμα ἀκούειν.[1]

A. F. POLLARD.

---

[1] Thucydides, bk. i. cp. 22: 'everlasting possessions, not prize compositions which are heard and forgotten.' (Jowett's translation.)

I

KILLING NO MURDER

[This pamphlet, the authorship of which was claimed by Colonel Silas Titus (1622-1704), was written by Colonel Edward Sexby, an officer in Cromwell's regiment during the Civil War, who, after becoming a Fifth Monarchy man and opposing Cromwell's Protectorate, was won over by the Royalists, fled to Holland and entered into various plots against the Protector's life. 'Killing no Murder' was published at Amsterdam in 1657, and was widely distributed in England. Sexby soon afterwards returned to England with the deliberate intention of assassinating Cromwell; he was arrested and died in the Tower in January 1658.][1]

TO

HIS HIGHNESS OLIVER CROMWELL.

MAY IT PLEASE YOUR HIGHNESS,

How I have spent some hours of the leisure your Highness hath been pleased to give me this following paper will give your Highness an account. How you will please

[1] See Introduction, p. 28.

to interpret it I cannot tell; but I can with confidence say, my intention in it is to procure your Highness that justice nobody yet does you, and to let the people see the longer they defer it the greater injury they do both themselves and you. To your Highness justly belongs the honour of dying for the people; and it cannot choose but be unspeakable consolation to you in the last moments of your life to consider with how much benefit to the world you are like to leave it. It is then only, my Lord, the titles you now usurp will be truly yours; you will then be indeed the deliverer of your country, and free it from a bondage little inferior to that from which Moses delivered his. You will then be that true reformer which you would be thought. Religion shall be then restored, liberty asserted, and Parliaments have those privileges they have fought for. We shall then hope that other laws will have place besides those of the sword, and that justice shall be otherwise defined than the will and pleasure of the strongest; and we shall then hope men will keep oaths again, and not have the necessity of being false and perfidious to preserve themselves, and be like their rulers. All this we hope from your Highness's happy expiration, who are the true father of your country; for while you live we can call nothing ours, and it is from your death that we hope for our inheritances. Let this consideration arm and fortify your Highness's mind against the fears of death, and the terrors of your evil conscience, that the good you will do by your death will something balance the evils of your life. And if in the black catalogue of high malefactors few can be found that have lived more to the affliction and disturbance of mankind than your Highness hath done, yet your greatest enemies will not deny but there are likewise as few that have expired more to the universal benefit of mankind than your Highness is like to do. To hasten this great good is the chief end of my writing this paper; and if it have the effects I hope it will, your Highness will quickly be out of the reach of men's malice, and your enemies will only be able to wound you in your memory, which strokes you will not feel. That your Highness may be speedily in this security is the universal wishes of your grateful country. This is the desire and prayer of the good and of the bad, and it may be is the only thing wherein all sects and factions do agree in their devotions, and is our only common prayer. But amongst all that put in their requests and supplications for your Highness's speedy deliverance from all earthly troubles, none is more assiduous nor more fervent than he who, with the rest of the nation, hath the honour to be,

May it please your Highness,
Your Highness's present slave and vassal,
W. A.[1]

[2] *I.e.* William Allen the pseudonym Sexby assumed.

II

A ROUGH DRAFT OF A NEW MODEL AT SEA

[This pamphlet by George Savile, Marquis of Halifax, is said to have been written in the autumn of 1667. The destruction of the ships of war at Chatham by the Dutch in the previous June had directed public attention to the scandalous condition of the navy. But though circulated in manuscript the pamphlet was not published until 1694 on the occasion of the introduction of a bill for the better discipline of the fleet, and it had certainly been recast since its original composition. It is remarkable as indicating the first essential of England's naval policy, and the advice 'Look to your Moat' is as pregnant to-day as in 1694. But the method in which Halifax incidentally deals with the broader questions of politics establishes his claim to be considered a pioneer in the scientific treatment of the subject.][1]

I WILL make no other Introduction to the following discourse, than that, as the importance of our being strong at *Sea*, was ever very great, so in our present circumstances it is grown to be much greater; because, as

[1] See *English Historical Review*, Oct. 1896, pp. 704-5, 722-26.

formerly our force of shipping contributed greatly to our *Trade* and safety, so, now it is become indispensably necessary to our very being.

It may be said now to *England, Martha, Martha*, thou art busy among many things, but one thing is necessary to the question, What shall we do to be saved in this world? There is no other answer but this, Look to your moat.

The first article of an *English-mans* Political creed must be, That he believeth in the Sea &c., without that, there needeth no General Council to pronounce him incapable of Salvation here.

We are in an Island confin'd to it by God Almighty, not as a penalty but a grace, and one of the greatest that can be given to mankind. Happy confinement that has made us free, rich and quiet; a fair portion in this world, and very well worth preserving, a figure that hath ever been envied, and could never be imitated by our neighbours. Our situation hath made Greatness abroad by land-conquests unnatural things to us. It is true, we made excursions, and glorious ones too, which made our names great in History, but they did not last.

Admit the *English* to be giants in courage, yet they must not hope to succeed in making war against Heaven, which seemeth to have enjoined them to acquiesce in being happy within their own Circle. It is no paradox to say, that *England* hath its root in the sea, and a deep one too, from whence it sendeth its branches into both the *Indies*.

We may say further in our present case, That if *allegiance* is due to *protection*, ours to the sea is due from that rule, since by that, and by that alone, we are to be protected; and if we have of late suffered usurpation of other methods, contrary to the homage we owe to that which must preserve us, it is time now to restore the *sea* to its right; and as there is no repentance effectual without amendment, so there is not a moment to be lost in the going about it.

It is not pretended to launch into such a voluminous treatise, as to set down everything to which so comprehensive a subject might lead me; for as the sea hath little less variety in it than the land; so the naval force of *England* extendeth itself into a great many branches, each of which are important enough to require a discourse apart, and peculiarly applied to it : but there must be preference to some consideration above others, when the weight of them is so visibly superior that it cannot be contested. It is there, first that the foundations are to be laid of our naval economy: amongst these, there is one article which in its own nature must be allowed to be the cornerstone of the building.

The choice of *Officers*, with the *discipline* and *encouragement* belonging to them. Upon this head only, I shall then take the liberty to venture my Opinion into the world, with a real submission to those, who may offer anything better for the advantage of the *public*.

The first question then will be, out of what sort of men the *Officers* of the *fleet* are to be chosen; and this immediately leadeth us to the present controversy between the *Gentlemen* and the *Tarpaulins*.[1]

The usual objection on both sides are too

---

[1] This term was applied to professional seamen risen from the ranks, a class which practically came into existence during the Commonwealth and contributed materially to its naval successes. They were systematically discouraged after the Restoration, when commands were habitually given to courtiers who had never been to sea in their lives. The natural result was defeat and disaster; and the question Halifax discusses which now seems idle was then a very practical one. See *English Historical Review*, January 1896.

general to be relied upon. Partiality and common prejudices direct most men's opinions, without entering into the particular reasons which ought to be the ground of it. There is so much ease in acquiescing in Generals, that the ignorance of those who cannot distinguish, and the laziness of those who will not, maketh men very apt to decline the trouble of stricter enquiries, which they think too great a price for being in the right, let it be never so valuable.

This maketh them judge in the lump, and either let their opinions swim along with the stream of the world, or give them up wholly to be directed by success. The effect of this is, that they change their minds upon every present uneasiness, wanting a steady foundation upon which their judgment should be formed. This is a perching upon the twigs of things, and not going to the root. But sure the matter in question deserveth to be examined in another manner, since so much dependeth upon it.

To state the thing impartially, it must be owned that it seemeth to lie fairest for the *Tarpaulin*: it giveth an impression that must have so much weight as to make a man's opinion lean very much on that side, it carrieth so much authority with it, it seemeth to be so unquestionable, that those are fittest to command at sea, who have not only made it their *calling*, but their *element;* that there must naturally be a prejudice to anything there can be said against it. There must therefore be some reason extraordinary to support the argument on the other side, or else the gentlemen could never enter the lists against such a violent objection, which seemeth not to be resisted. I will introduce my argument with an assertion, which as I take it to be true almost in all cases, so it is necessary to be explained and enforced in this. The *assertion* is, that there is hardly a single proposition to be made, which is not deceitful, and the tying our reason too close to it, may in many cases be destructive. Circumstances must come in, and are to be made a part of the matter of which we are to judge; positive *decisions* are always dangerous more especially in *politics*. A man, who will be master of an argument, must do like a skilful General, who sendeth scouts on all sides, to see whether there may not be an enemy. So he must look round to see what objections can be made, and not go in a straight line, which is the ready way to lead him into a mistake.

Before then, that we conclude what sort of

men are fitted to command at sea, a principle is to be laid down, that there is a differing consideration to be had of such a subject-matter, as is in itself distinct and independent, and of such a one as being a limit of a body, or a wheel of a frame, there is a necessity of suiting it to the rest and preserving the harmony of the whole. A man must not in that case restrain himself to the separate consideration of that single part, but must take care it may fall in and agree with the shape of the whole creature, of which it is a member. According to this proposition, which I take to be indisputable, it will not I hope appear an affectation, or an extravagant fit of unreasonable politics, if, before I enter into the particular state of the present question, I say something of the government of *England,* and make that the groundwork of what sort of men are most proper to be made use of to command at sea.

The forms of government to which *England* must be subjected, are either *Absolute Monarchy,* a *Commonwealth,*[1] or a *Mixt Monarchy,*[2] as it is now; with those natural alterations that the exigency of affairs may from time to time suggest. As to absolute monarchy, I will not

---

[1] 'Republic' would now be the usual term.
[2] Limited Monarchy.

allow myself to be transported into such invectives, as are generally made against it;[1] neither am I ready to enter into the aggravating style of calling everything *slavery*, that restraineth men in any part of their freedom: one may discern in this, as in most other things, the good and bad of it. We see by too near an instance, what *France* doth by it; it doth not only struggle with the rest of *Christendom*, but is in a fair way of giving law to it.[2]

This is owing in great measure to a *despotic* and undivided power; the uncontrolable authority of the directive councils maketh everything move without disorder or opposition, which must give an advantage, that is plain enough of itself,[3] without being proved by the melancholy experience we have of it at this time.

I see and admire this; yet I consider at the same time, that all things of this kind are comparative: that as on one side, without *Government*, men cannot enjoy what belongeth to them in particular, nor can a nation be secure,

---

[1] A singular illustration of the detachment with which Halifax treated the burning political questions of his day.

[2] This passage alluding to the dangerous supremacy of Louis XIV. must have been introduced in 1694.

[3] An advantage which still creates a desire in certain minds for the introduction of the Russian administrative system into England.

or preserve itself in general; so, on the other side, the end of *Government* being that Mankind should live in some competent state of freedom, it is very unnatural to have the *end* destroyed by the *means* that were originally made use of to attain it. In this respect something is to be ventured, rather than submit to such a precarious state of life, as would make it a burden to a reasonable creature; and therefore, after I have owned the advantages in some kind of an unlimited government; yet, while they are attended with so many other discouraging circumstances, I cannot think but that they may be bought too dear; and if it should be so, that it is not possible for a *state* to be *great* and *glorious*, unless the subjects are *wretchedly miserable*. I am ashamed to own my low-spirited frailty, in preferring such a model of government, as may agree with the reasonable enjoyment of a *free people*, before such a one, by which empire is to be extended at such an unnatural price. Besides, whatever men's opinions may be one way or another, in the general question, there is an argument in our case that shutteth the door to any answer to it (viz.), We cannot subsist under a *despotic* power, our very being would be destroyed by it; for we are to consider, we are a very little spot in the map of the world, and make a great figure only by *trade*, which is the creature of liberty; one destroyed, the other falleth to the ground by a natural consequence, that will not admit a dispute. If we would be measured by our acres, we are a poor inconsiderable people; we are exalted above our natural bounds, by our good laws, and our excellent constitution. By this we are not only happy at home, but considerable abroad. Our situation, our humour, our trade, do all concur to strengthen this argument. So that all other reasons must give place to such a one as maketh it out, that there is no mean between a *Free Nation* and *No Nation*.

We are no more a people, nor *England* can no longer keep its name from the moment that our liberties are extinguished; the vital strength that should support us being withdrawn, we should then be no more than a carcass of a nation, with no other security than that of *contempt;* and to subsist on no other tenure, than that we should be below the giving temptation to our stronger neighbours to devour us. In my judgment, therefore, there is such a short decision to be made upon this subject, that in relation to *England* an *Absolute Monarchy* is as an unreasonable thing to be wished, as I hope it will be impossible to be obtained.

It must be considered in the next place, whether *England* is likely to be turned into a commonwealth. It is hard at any time to determine what will be the shape of the next Revolution, much more at this time would it be inexcusably arrogant to undertake it. Who can foresee whether it will be from without, or from within, or from both? Whether with or without the concurrence of the people? Whether regularly produced, or violently imposed? I shall not therefore *magisterially* declare it impossible that a Commonwealth should be settled here; but I may give my humble opinion, that according to all appearances, it is very improbable.[1]

I will first lay it down for a principle, That it is not a sound way of arguing to say, That if it can be made out, that the form of a Commonwealth will best suit with the interest of the nation, it must for that reason of necessity prevail.

I will not deny but that Interest will not lie, is a right Maxim, where ever it is sure to be

[1] This, again, was probably written after the Revolution; otherwise, taken with the assumption that there would be another Revolution, it was a remarkable prophecy.

understood; else one had as good affirm, That no man in particular, nor Mankind in general, can ever be mistaken. A nation is a great while before they can see, and generally they must feel first before their sight is quite cleared. This *maketh* it so long before they can see their *Interest*, that for the most part it is too late for them to pursue it: if men must be supposed always to follow their true *interest*, it must be meant of a new manufactory of Mankind by God Almighty: there must be some new *clay*, the old *stuff* never yet made any such infallible creature.

This being premised, it is to be inquired, Whether instead of inclination, or a leaning towards a *Commonwealth*, there is not in *England* a general dislike to it; if this be so as I take it to be by a very great disparity in numbers; it will be in vain to dispute the *reason*, whilst humour is against it, allowing the weight that is due to the argument, which may be alleged for it; yet, if the herd is against it, the going about to convince them, would have no other effect than to show that nothing can be more impertinent than good *reasons*, when they are misplaced or ill-timed.

I must observe, that there must be some previous dispositions in all great changes to facilitate and to make way for them: I think it not at all absurd, I affirm, That such resolutions are seldom made at all except by the general preparations of men's minds they are half made before, and it is plainly visible, that men go about them.

Though it seemeth to me that the argument alone maketh all others unnecessary, yet I must take notice that besides what hath been said on this subject, there are certain preliminaries to the first building a Commonwealth. Some materials absolutely necessary for the carrying on such a fabric which at present are wanting amongst us, I mean *Virtue, Morality, Diligence,* or at least *Hypocrisy.* Now this age is so plain dealing, as not to dissemble so far as to an outward pretence of *qualities* which seem at present so *unfashionable,* and under so much discountenance.

From hence we may draw a plain and natural inference, that a *Commonwealth* is not fit for us, because we are not fit for a *Commonwealth.*

This being granted, the supposition of this form of government of *England,* with all its consequences as to the present question, must be excluded, and *Absolute Monarchy* having been seen so far by the reasons at once alleged, it will without further examinations fall to a *Mixt Government,* as we now are. I will not say, that there is never to be any alteration; the constitution of the several parts that concur to make up the frame of the present Government, may be altered in many things, in some for the better, and in others, perhaps for the worse, according as circumstances shall arise to induce a *change;* and as passion and interest shall have more or less influence upon the public councils; but still, if it remaineth in the whole so far a *mixt Monarchy,* that there shall be a restraint upon the *Prince,* as to the exercise of a *despotic power,* it is enough to make a ground work for the present question. It appeareth then that a *bounded Monarchy* is that kind of Government which will most probably prevail and continue in *England;* from whence it must follow (as hath been hinted before) that every considerable part ought to be so composed, as the better to conduce to the preserving the harmony of the whole constitution.[1] The *navy* is of so great importance, that it would be disparaged by calling it less than the *life* and *soul* of government.

---

[1] An anticipation in some measure of Burke's favourite dogma of the "balance of the constitution."

Therefore to apply the argument to the subject we are upon; in case the *Officers* be all *Tarpaulins*, it would be in reality too great a tendency to a *Commonwealth;* such a part of the constitution being democratically disposed may be suspected to endeavour to bring it into that shape; where the influence must be so strong, and the supposition will be the more justifiable. In short, if the *Maritime Force*, which is the only thing that can defend us, should be wholly directed by the lower sort of men, with an entire exclusion of the *nobility* and *gentry;* it will not be so easy to answer the arguments supported by so great a probability, that such a scheme would not only lean toward a *democracy*, but directly lead us into it.[1]

Let us now examine the contrary proposition, (viz.) *that all officers should be gentlemen.*

Here the objection lieth so fair of its introducing an *arbitrary government*, that it as little to be answered in that respect, as the former is in the other. *Gentlemen*, in a general definition, will be suspected to lie more than other men, under the temptations of being made instruments of unlimited power; their relations, their way of living, their taste of the entertainments

---

[1] Halifax alludes to the fact that during the Civil War the navy was preponderantly anti-royalist.

of the Court, inspire an Ambition that generally draweth their inclination towards it, besides the gratifying of their interests. Men of quality are often taken with the ornaments of government, the splendour dazzleth them so, as that their judgments are surprised by it; and there will be always some that have so little remorse for invading other men's liberties, that it maketh them less solicitous to preserve their own.

These things throw them naturally into such a dependance as might give a dangerous bias; if they alone were in command at sea, it would make the great wheel turn by an irregular motion, and instead of being the chief means of preserving the whole frame, might come to be the chief instruments to discompose and dissolve it.

The two further exclusive propositions being necessarily to be excluded in this question, there remaineth no other expedient; neither can any other conclusion be drawn from the argument as it hath been stated, than that there must be a mixture in the navy of *Gentlemen* and *Tarpaulins*, as there is in the constitution of the government, of power and liberty. This mixture is not to be so rigorously defined, as to set down the exact proportion there is to be of each; the greater or lesser number must be directed by circumstances, of which the government is to judge, and which makes it improper to set such bounds, as that on no occasion it shall on either side be lessened or enlarged. It is possible the men of *Wapping* may think they are injured, by giving them any partners in the dominion of the *sea;* they may take it unkindly to be jostled in their own *element* by men of such a different education, that they may be said to be of another species; they will be apt to think it an usurpation upon them, and notwithstanding the influences that are against them, and which give a kind of prescription on the other side, they will not easily acquiesce in what they conceive to be a hardship to them.

But I shall in a good measure reconcile myself to them by what follows; (viz.) The *Gentlemen* shall not be capable of bearing office at *sea*, except they be *Tarpaulins* too; that is to say, except they are so trained up by a continued habit of living at *sea*, that they may have a right to be admitted free *denizens* of *Wapping*. Upon this dependeth the whole matter; and indeed here lieth the difficulty, because the *Gentlemen* brought up under the connivance of a looser discipline, and of an easier admittance, will take it heavily to be reduced within the *Fetters* of such a *New Model*;[1] and I conclude they will be extremely averse to that which they call an unreasonable yoke upon them, that their original consent is never to be expected. But if it appeareth to be convenient, and which is more, that it is necessary for the preservation of the whole that it should be so, the Government must be called upon in aid to suppress these first boilings of discontent; the rules must be imposed with such authority, and the execution of them must be so well supported, that by degrees their impatience will be subdued, and they will concur in an establishment to which they will every day be more reconciled.

They will find it will take away the objections which are now thrown upon them, of setting up for masters without having even been apprentices; or at least without having served out their time.

Mankind naturally swelleth against favour and partiality; their belief of their own merit maketh men object them to a prosperous competitor, even when there is no pretence for it; but when there is the least handle offered, to be sure it will be taken. So, in this case,

[1] An allusion of course to Cromwell's 'New Model.'

when a *Gentleman* is preferred at *sea* the *Tarpaulin* is very apt to impute it to friend or favour; but if that *Gentleman* hath before his preferment passed through all the steps which lead to it, that he smelleth as much of *pitch* and *tar*, as though that were *swaddled* in *sailcloth;* his having an *escutcheon* will be so far from doing him harm, that it will set him upon the advantage ground: it will draw a real respect to his quality when so supported, and give him an influence, and authority infinitely superior to that which the *mere seaman* can never pretend to.

When a *Gentleman* hath learned how to *obey*, he will grow very much fitter to *command;* his own Memory will advise him not to command too rigorous punishments. He will better resist the temptations of authority (which are great) when he reflecteth how much he hath at other times wished it might be gently exercised, when he was liable to the rigour of it.

When the undistinguished *Discipline* of a ship hath tamed the young mastership, which is apt to arise from a *Gentleman's* birth and education, he then groweth proud in the right place, and valueth himself first upon knowing his duty, and then upon doing it.

In plain *English*, men of *Quality* in their

several degrees must either restore themselves to a better opinion, both for *Morality* and *Diligence,* or else *Quality* itself will be in danger of being extinguished.

The original *Gentleman* is almost lost in strictness, when posterity doth not still further adorn by their virtue. The escutcheon their ancestors first got for them by their merit, they deserve the penalty of being deprived of it.

To expect that *Quality* alone should waft men up into *Places* and *Employments,* is as unreasonable, as to think that a ship, because it is carved and gilded, should be fit to go to *sea* without *sails* or *tackling.* But when a *Gentleman* maketh no other use of his *quality,* than to incite him the more to his duty, it will give such a true and settled *superiority,* as must destroy all competition from those that are below him.

It is time now to go to the probationary qualifications of an *officer* at *sea:* and I have some to offer, which I have digested in my thoughts, I hope impartially, that they may not be speculative notions, but things easy and practicable, if the directing powers will give due countenance and encouragement to the execution of them: but whilst I am going about to set them down, though this little *essay* was made to no other *end*, than to introduce them, I am upon better recollection, induced to put a restraint upon myself, and rather retract the promise I made at the beginning than by advising the particular methods, by which I conceive the good *end* that is aimed at may be obtained, to incur the imputation of the thing of the world, of which I would least be guilty, which is of anticipating, by my private opinion, the judgment of the *Parliament*, or seeming out of my slender stock of reason to dictate to the supreme wisdom of the nation. They will, no doubt, consider the present establishments for *discipline* at *sea*, which are many of them very good, and if well executed, might go a great way in the present question. But I will not say they are so perfect, but that other may be added to make them more effectual, and that some more supplemental expedients may be necessary to complete what is yet defective: and whenever the *Parliament* shall think fit to take this matter into their consideration, I am sure they will not want for their direction, the auxiliary reasons of any man without doors, much less of one, whose thoughts are so entirely and unaffectedly resigned to whatever they shall determine in this, or any thing else relating to the Public.

III

SOME CAUTIONS FOR CHOICE OF MEMBERS OF PARLIAMENT

[This pamphlet was written by Halifax in 1695, a short while before his death and soon after the passing of the Triennial Act. It is full of polished irony and illustrates Halifax's contempt for both political parties; at the same time it contains a great deal of incidental information about politics and manners of the time.]

I WILL make no other introduction, than that it is hoped the Counties and Boroughs will remember in general, that besides other consequences, they will have the credit of a good choice, or the scandal that belongeth to an ill one.

The creators will be thought like their creatures; and therefore an ill choice will either be a disparagement of their understanding or their morals.

There cannot be a fuller approbation of a thing, than the choosing of it; so that the fault of the members chosen, if known beforehand, will be judged to be of the growth of that County or Borough, after such a solemn approbation of them.

In short, those who send up their representatives to *Westminster*, should take care they may be such as will do them right, and their Country honour.

Now to the particulars.

I. A very extraordinary earnestness to be chosen is no very good symptom: A desire to serve the Nation in Parliament is an *English* man's ambition: always to be encouraged, and never to be disapproved.

A man may not only be willing to stand, but he may declare that willingness to his friends, that they may assist him, and by all the means becoming a modest and prudent man, he may endeavour to succeed, and prevent the being disappointed in it.

But there is a wide difference between this and the raising a kind of petty war in the County or Corporation, entering the lists rather for a combat than an election; throwing fireballs to put men into heat, and omitting to spread no reports, whether true or false, which may give an advantage by laying a blemish upon a competitor.

These methods will ever be suspicious; it will never be thought a natural thing for men to take such extravagant pains for the mere sake of doing good to others.

To be content to suffer something for a good end, is that which many would do without any great repugnance: but where a man can honestly propose nothing to himself except troubles, change and loss by absence from his own affairs, to be violent in the pursuit of so ill a bargain is not at all suited to the languishing virtue of Mankind so corrupted.

Such a self-denying zeal in such a self-seeking age, is so little to be imagined, that it may without injury be suspected.

Therefore when these blustering pretenders come upon the Stage, their natural temper and other circumstances ought to be very well considered, before men trust them with the disposal of their money, or their liberty.

And I am apt to believe, there could hardly be found one single man whose other Qualifications would over-balance the objections that lie against such importunate suitors.

II. Recommending letters ought to have no effect upon elections.

In this I must distinguish; for though in strictness perhaps there should be no exceptions; yet in compliance with long practice, and out of an Indulgence that is necessary in a time when Mankind is too much loosened from severe rules, to be kept close up to them, letters sent only from equal men, doing good men right by giving evidence in their behalf, offering them as fitly qualified, when they really are so, and freeing them from unjust aspersions, may still be allowed.

The letters I mean, are from men of power, where it may be beneficial to comply, and inconvenient to oppose.

Choice must not only be free from force, but from Influence, which is a degree of force: there must be no difficulty, no apprehension that a refusal will be ill taken or resented.

The freeholders must be freemen too; they are to have no shackles upon their votes in an election: and the men who stand, should carry their own letters of recommendation about them, which are their good character and behaviour in the world, without borrowing evidence, especially when it comes from suspected hands.

Those who make use of these epistles, ought to have no more advantage from them, than the *Muscovites* have from the letters put into their hands, when they are buried, to recommend them to *St Nicholas*.

The first should get as little admittance for

men into the Parliament, as these letters can introduce the bearers into Heaven.

The scandal of such letters lieth first in the arrogant imposing of those that write them, and next in the wretched meanness of those that need them.

Men must have fallen very low in their credit, who upon such an occasion have a recourse to power to support it: their enemies could not give stronger evidence of their not being fit for that which they pretend to. And if the electors judge otherwise they will be pretty sure in a little time to see their mistake, and to repent it.

III. Non-attendance in former parliaments ought to be a bar against the choice of men who have been guilty of it.

It is one of the worst kinds of non-residence, and the least to be excused: it is very hard that men should despise a duty, which perhaps is the only ground of the respect that is paid to them.

It is such a piece of sauciness for any one to press for the honour of serving in Parliament, and then to be careless in attending it, that in a House where there were so many officers, the penalty had not been improper to have cashiered them for not appearing at the general muster.

If men forbear to come out of laziness let them be gratified by taking their ease at home without interruption: if out of small cunning to avoid difficulties, and to escape from the inconvenience of voting in critical cases, let them enjoy that despicable pitch of wisdom, and never pretend to make a figure where the public is to be served.

If it would be thought advisable to trust a man immediately after he hath been drawn out of gaol, it may be as reasonable to look upon one who for his non-attendance in the House hath been for in custody, as a kind of bankrupt, which putteth him upon unequal terms with those who have been assiduous in the discharge of their duty.

They who thought fit in one session to neglect the Public business, may be justly suspected by their own standing, in the next to intend their own.

Besides these more deliberate offenders, there are some who do not attend even when they are in the House; absent in their thoughts for want of comprehending the business that is doing, and therefore diverted from it by anything that is trivial.

Such men are nuisances to a serious assembly, and when they are numerous it amounteth almost to a Dissolution, it being scarce possible for good sense to be heard, whilst a noise is made by the buzzing of these horse flies.

The *Roman* censors who degraded a senator for yawning whilst there was a debate would have much more abundant matter here upon which they might exercise their jurisdiction.

To conclude this head, there are so few that ever mended in these cases, that after the first experiment it is not at all reasonable to take them upon a new trial.

IV. Men who are unquiet and busy in their natures, are to give more than ordinary proofs of their integrity, before the electing them into a public trust can be justified. As a hot summer breedeth greater swarms of flies, so an active time breedeth a greater number of these shining Gentlemen.

It is pretty sure, that men who cannot allow themselves to be at rest, will let nobody else be quiet. Such a perpetual activity is apt by degrees to be applied to the pursuit of their private interest. And their thoughts being in a continual motion, they have not time to dwell long enough upon anything to entertain a scruple.

So that they are generally at full liberty to do what is most convenient for them, without being fettered by any restraints.

Nay further; whenever it happeneth that there is an impunity for cheating, these nimble gentlemen are apt to think it a disparagement to their understandings not to go into it.

I doubt it is not a wrong to the present age, to say, that a knave is a less unpopular calling than it hath been in former times. And to say truth, it would be ingratitude in some men to turn honest when they owe all they have to their knavery.

The people are in this respect unhappy; they are too many to do their own business; their numbers, which make their strength, are at the same time the cause of their weakness; they are too unwieldy to move; and for this reason nothing can ever redeem them from this incurable impotency: so that they must have solicitors to pursue and look after their interests; who are too often disposed to dispense with the fidelity they owe to those that trust them; especially if the Government will pay their bills without abatement.

It is better these gentlemen's dexterity should be employed anywhere than in Parliament, where the ill consequences of their being Members is too much diffused, and not restrained to the County or Borough who shall be so unwary as to choose them.

V. Great drinkers are less fit to serve in Parliament than is apprehended.

Men's virtue, as well as their understanding, is apt to be tainted by it.

The appearance of it is sociable and well-natured, but it is by no means to be relied upon.

Nothing is more frail than a man too far engaged in wet popularity.

The habit of it maketh men careless of their business, and that naturally leadeth them into circumstances, that make them liable to temptation.

It is seldom seen, that any principles have such a root, as that they can be proof against the continual droppings of a bottle.

As to the faculties of the mind, there is not less objection; the vapours of wine may sometimes throw out sparks of Wit, but they are like scattered pieces of ore, there is no vein to work upon.

Such wit, even the best of it, is like paying great fines; in which case there must of necessity be an abatement of the constant rent.

Nothing sure is a greater enemy to the brain, than too much moisture; it can the least of anything bear the being continually steeped: and it may be said, that thought may be resembled to some creatures which can live only in a dry country.

Yet so arrogant are some men, as to think they are so much masters of business, as that they can play with it; they imagine they can drown their reason once a day, and that it shall not be the worse for it; forgetting, that by too often diving, the understanding at last groweth too weak to rise up again.

I will suppose this fault was less frequent when *Solon* made it one of his laws, that it was lawful to kill a magistrate if he was found drunk. Such a liberty taken in this age, either in Parliament or out of it, would do terrible execution.

I cannot but mention a Petition in the year 1647 from the County of *Devon*, to the House of Commons, against the undue election of Burgesses, who are strong in wine and weak in wisdom.

The cause of such petitions is to be prevented by choosing such as shall not give handle for them.

VI. Wanting-men[1] give such cause of suspicion wherever they deal, that surely the choosers will be on their guard, as often as such dangerous pretenders make their application to them.

[1] *I.e.* men in want or of slender means.

Let the behaviour of such men be never so plausible and untainted, yet they who are to pitch upon those they are to trust with all they have, may be excused, if they do not consider what they are but what they may be.

As we pray ourselves we may not be led into temptation, we ought not by any means to thrust others into it; even though our own interest was not concerned; and sure when it is, the argument hath not less force.

If a man hath a small estate, and a numerous family; where it happeneth that a man hath as many children as he hath tenants, it is not a recommending circumstance for his election.

When it cometh to be the question with such a man, whether he shall be just to the public, or cruel to his family? it is very possible the decision may be on the side of corrupted nature.

It is a compliment to this age, which it doth not deserve, to suppose men are so tied up to Morality, as that they cannot be pinched out of it; especially now when it is called starving not to be embroidered or served in plate.

The men chosen to serve their Country, should not be loaded with suits that may tempt them to assume privileges; much less under such necessities as may more immediately prepare them for corruption.

Men who need a Parliament for their own particular interest, have more reason to offer their service than others have to accept of it. And though I do not doubt, but there are some whose virtue would triumph over their wants, let them be never so pressing, to expose the public to the hazard of being deceived, is that which can never be justified by those that choose. And though it must be allowed possible for a wanting-man to be honest, yet it is impossible for a man to be wise that will depend on it.

VII. There is a sort of men that have a tinsel-wit, which make them shine among those who cannot judge.

Club and coffee house gentlemen, petty merchants of small conceits, who have an empty habit of prating without meaning; they always aim at wit and generally make false fire.

Their business is less to learn, than to set themselves out; which makes them choose to be with such as can only be witnesses of their small ingenuity, rather than with such as might improve it.

There is a subordinate wit, as much inferior

to a wit of business, as a fiddler at a Wake is to the lofty sound of the organ.

Men of this size are in no degree suited to the business of redressing grievances and making laws.

There is a Parliament wit to be distinguished from all other kinds; those who have it, do not stuff their heads only with cavils and objections.

They have a deliberate and an observing wit, a head turned to public things; men who place greater pleasure in mending a fault than in finding it out.

Their understanding directeth them to object in the right place and not like those who go by no other rule, than to conclude, that must be the best counsel which was not taken.

These wholesale judges show such a gross and peevish ignorance that it appeareth so openly in all they say or do, that they give loud warning to all considering men, not to choose them.

VIII. The dislike of slight airy men must not go so far, as to recommend heaviness in opposition to it, especially where men are convicted of it by experience in former sessions.

As a lively coxcomb will seldom fail to lay in his claim for wit; so a blockhead is apt to pretend, that his heaviness is a proof of his judgement.

Some have a universal lethargy spread upon their understanding without exception; others have an insufficiency *quoad hoc,* these last can never so turn their thoughts to public business, as to give the attention that is necessary to comprehend it.

There are those who have such a thick shell upon their brains, that their ignorance is impenetrable, and maketh such a stout resistance against common sense, that it will never be subdued by it: true heart of oak, ignorance that will never yield, let reason beat never so hard upon it; and though their kind neighbours have at several elections sent them up to school again, they have still returned the same incurable dunces.

There is a false gravity that is a very ill symptom; and it may be said, that as rivers, which run very slowly, have always the most mud at the bottom; so a solid stiffness in the constant course of a man's life, is a sign of a thick bed of mud at the bottom of his brain.

A dull man is so near a dead man, that he is hardly to be ranked in the list of the living; and as he is not to be buried whilst he is half alive, so he is as little to be employed whilst he is half dead.

Parliaments are now grown to be quite other things than they were formerly.

In ancient times they were little more than great Assizes; a roll of grievances *Magna Charta* confirmed; privileges of Holy Church preserved; so many sacks of wool given, and away.

Now there are traps and gins laid for the well meaning Country-gentleman; he is to grapple with the cunning of Men in Town, which is not a little improved by being rewarded and encouraged.

So that men whose good intentions are not seconded and supported by some degree of ability, are much the more dangerous, as they are less criminal than cunning knaves. Their honest mistakes, for want of distinguishing, either give a countenance to, or at least lessen the scandal of the injurious things that are done to the public: and with leave asked for so odd an expression, their innocent guilt is as mischievous to the laws and liberties, as the most deliberate malice of those that would destroy them.[1]

[1] It has since become a platitude that in politics blunders are crimes: *cf.* Talleyrand's remark, "it was worse than a crime, it was a blunder."

IX. There is an abuse which daily increaseth, of sending such to Parliament, as are scarce old enough to be sent to the University.

I would not in this restrain the definition of these boys to the age of twenty-one: if my opinion might take place, I should wish that none might be chosen into the House of Commons under thirty; and to make some equality, I should from the same motives think it convenient, that no lord should have a vote in judicature under that age.

But to leave this digression; I cannot see why the choosers should not at least make it a rule among themselves; not to send any man to represent them under the age of twenty-five, which is the time of majority in most other places of the world. Surely it is not that we are earlier plants than our neighbours. Such supposition could neither be justified by our climate, nor by the degree of latitude in which we are placed; I must therefore attribute it to the haste our Ancestors had (and not without reason) to free themselves from the severity of wardships.

But whether this, or anything else, was the cause of our earlier stepping into man's estate; so it is now, that according to our laws, twenty-one is the age of discretion; and the young man is then vested with a legal, how defective soever he may be in his natural, understanding.

With all this, there ought to be a difference made between coming out of pupilage, and leaping into legislatorship.

It is perhaps inconvenient enough that a man should be so soon let loose to destroy his own estate; but it is yet worse, that he should then have the power of giving away other men's.

The law must make general rules, to which there always will be some objections.

If there were tryers appointed to judge when leading-strings should be left off, many would wear them a very great while, and some perhaps with their grey hairs; there being no small number of old boys in all times and especially in this.

It is necessary therefore to make exceptions to this general rule, where the case so much requireth it, as it doth in the matter in question.

The ground of sending these *Minors* to Parliament ought not to recommend the continuance of it to those who are lovers of liberty; since it was by the authority and influence of great men, that their stripling sons were first received by the humble depending Boroughs, or the complying Counties.

They called it, as many do still, the best school for young men. Now experience hath showed us, that it is like a school only in this respect, that these youngsters when they are admitted deserve to be whipped in it.

If the House of Commons is a school, it must be for men of riper age; these are too young to learn there, and being elevated by a mistaken smattering in small politics, they grow too supercilious to learn anywhere else; so that instead of improving young promising plants, they are destroyed by being misplaced. If then they do themselves hurt by it, it is surer yet that they do the House no good by coming into it.[1]

They were not green geese that are said to have saved the Capitol; they were certainly of full age, or else their cackling could not have been heard, so as to give warning.

Indeed it looked of late, when the fashion was to have long continued parliaments,[2] as

[1] Halifax's rule would have excluded the younger Pitt from parliament for six years after he had become prime minister.

[2] The Long Parliament sat with various interruptions from 1640 to 1659. Charles II.'s first parliament sat from 1660 to 1679.

if we might plant a boy in the House with a prospect that he might continue there till he had grey hairs: and that the same sapling might have such a root, as that he might grow up to be timber without being removed.

If these young men had skill enough to pitch upon somebody in the House, to whom they might resign their opinion, and upon whose judgment they might lean without reserve, there might be less objection.

But to speak Truth, they know as little how to choose, as those did who elected them; so that there is no other expedient left, than the letting them alone.

One may say, generally speaking, that a young man being too soon qualified for the serious business of Parliaments, would really be no good symptom.

It is a sign of too much phlegm, and too little fire in the beginning of age if men have not a little more heat than is convenient; for as they grow older they will run a hazard of not having so much as is necessary.

The truth is, the vigour of youth is softened and misapplyed, when it is not spent either in war or close studies; all other courses have an idle mixture that cometh to nothing, and maketh them like trees, which for want of pruning run up to wood, and seldom or never bear any fruit.

To conclude this head, it must be owned, that there is no age of our life which doth not carry arguments along with it to humble us: and therefore it would be well for the business of the world, if young men would stay longer before they went into it, and old men not so long before they went out of it.

X. Next to these may be ranked a sort of superfine gentlemen, carpet-knights, men whose heads may be said to be only appurtenances to their perukes, which entirely engross all their care and application.

Their understanding is so strictly appropriated to their dress, that no part of it is upon pain of their utmost displeasure to be diverted to any other use.

It is not by this intended to recommend an affected clown, or to make it a necessary qualification for a member of Parliament, that he must renounce clean linen or good manners; but surely a too earnest application to make everything fit right about them, striketh too deep into their small stock of thoughts to allow it furniture for anything else.

To do right to these fine-spun gentlemen, business is too coarse a thing for them, which maketh it an unreasonable hardship upon them to oppress them with it; so that in tenderness to them, no less than out of care to the public, it is best to leave them to their tailors with whom they will live in much better correspondence, when the danger is prevented of their falling out about privileges.

XI. Men of injustice and violence, in their private dealings, are not to be trusted by the people with a commission to treat for them in Parliament.

In the 4*th* of *Edw.* III. The king commandeth in his Writs not to choose any Knights who had been guilty of crime, or maintenance.[1]

These warm men seldom fail to run into maintenance, taken in a larger extent.

It is an unnatural sound to come from a man that is arbitrary in his neighbourhood, to talk of laws and liberties at *Westminster;* he is not a proper vehicle for such words, which ought never to be prophaned.

[1] See Stubbs, *Constitutional History*, iii. 549 *et seq.*; maintenance was the practice of great men taking up the cause or quarrel of humbler persons on condition of exercising over them the rights of patron. It was open to many abuses and legislation against it was frequent. The most familiar effect of it was the gathering round the nobles of large bands of retainers who were a fruitful cause of disturbance.

An habitual breaker of the laws, to be made one of the law-makers, is as if the benches in *Westminster-hall* should be filled with men out of *Newgate*.

Those who are of this temper cannot change their nature out of respect to their country.

Quite contrary, they will less scruple to do wrong to a nation where nobody taketh it to himself, than to particular men to whose resentments they are more immediately exposed.

In short they lie under such strong objections, that the overbalance of better men cannot altogether purify an assembly where these unclean beasts are admitted.

XII. Excessive spenders and unreasonable savers are to be excluded, being both greedy from differing causes.

They are both of them diseases of infection, and for that reason are not to be admitted into public assemblies.

A prodigal man must be greedy because he thinketh he can never spend enough.

The wretch[1] must be so, because he will never think he can hoard enough.

The world first admireth men's wisdom for getting money and then raileth at them if

---

[1] *I.e.* 'miser': wretch is a literal translation of the Latin word 'miser.'

they do not throw it away. So that the prodigal man is only the less unpopular extreme; he is every jot as well prepared as the miser to fall out with his morals, when once a good temptation is offered him to lay them aside.

On the other side, some rich men are as eager to overtake those that are richer, as a running-horse is to get to the race-post, before the other that contendeth with him.

Men often desire to heap, rather because others have more, than that they know what to do with that which they covet with so much impatience.

So that it is plain, the fancy hath as great a share in this imaginary pleasure of gathering as it hath in love, ambition, or any other passion.

It is pretty sure, that as no man was ever the richer for having a good estate, if he did not look after it, so neither will he be the honester if he hath never so much.

Want of care will always create want of money; so that whether a man is a beggar because he never had any money, or because he can never keep any, it is all one to those who are to trust him.

Upon this head of prodigality, it may be no

unreasonable caution to be afraid of those who in former service have been extravagantly liberal of the public money.

Trusting is so hazardous a thing, that it should never be done but where it is necessary; so that when Trustees are found upon trial to be very lavish, even without examining into the causes of it (which are generally very suspicious), it is a reasonable part of preventing wit to change hands, or else the choosers will pay the penalty that belongeth to good nature so misplaced, and the consequences will be attended with the aggravation of their being made wiser by such a severe and costly warning.

XIII. It would be of very great use to take a general resolution throughout the kingdom, that none should be chosen for a county but such as have either in possession, or reversion, a considerable estate in it; nor for a Borough, except he be resiant[1] or that he hath some estate in the County, in present or expectancy.

There have been excellent men of law who

---

[1] Resident; originally it was the rule that members should be resident in the boroughs they represented. In 1571 it was proposed to repeal the old law altogether. In the debate that ensued it was asserted as a principle that a member was not the mere delegate of his constituents, and that he served for the whole kingdom, and not only for the body that chose him. The bill passed the Commons by a large majority but was then suffered

were of opinion, that in case of a burgess of a town not resiant, the court is to give judgment according to the statute,[1] notwithstanding custom to the contrary.

But not to insist now upon that, the prudential part is argument enough to set up a rule to abrogate an ill custom.

There is not, perhaps, a greater cause of the corruption of Parliaments, than by adopting Members, who may be said to have no title by their births.

The juries are by the law to be *Ex vicineto ;* and shall there be less care that the representatives of the people be so too?

Sure the interest of the County is best placed in the hands of such as have some share in it.

---

to drop. Nevertheless the old law ceased to be enforced. And it was well that it did, for the non-resident lawyers who became members rendered great service in the struggle with the crown. The renewal of it would be fatal, as it would exclude any man of ability from Parliament if he chanced to reside in a constituency of permanently hostile views to his own: *e.g.* no Liberal residing in the west end of London would be able to sit in Parliament.

[1] *I.e.* the statute of 1413, 1 Henry V. cp. 1, which directs that none be chosen knights, citizens, or burgesses, who are not resident within the place for which they are returned on the day of the date of the writ: see Hallam's *Middle Ages,* iii. 118, 119, and Stubbs's *Const. Hist.,* iii. 438.

The outliers are not so easily kept within the pale of the laws.

They are often chosen without being known, which is more like choosing valentines, than Members of Parliament. The motive of their standing is more justly to be supposed, that they may redress their own grievances which they know, than those of the Country to which they are strangers.

They are chosen at *London* to serve in *Cornwall*, &c., and are often Parties, before they come to be representatives : one would think the reproach it is for a County not to have men within their own circle to serve them in Parliament, should be argument enough to reject these trespassers, without urging the ill consequences in other respects of their being admitted.

XIV. As in some cases it is advisable to give a total exclusion to men not fitly qualified ; so in others it is more proper to lay down a general rule of caution, with allowance of some exceptions, where men have given such proofs of themselves, as create a right for them to be distinguished.

Of this nature is that which I shall say concerning lawyers, who, by the same reason that they may be useful, may be also very dangerous.

The negligence, and want of application in gentlemen, hath made them[1] to be thought more necessary than naturally they are in Parliament.

They have not only engrossed the Chair of the Speaker, but that of a Committee is hardly thought to be well filled, except it be by a man of the robe.

This maketh it worthy of the more serious reflection of all gentlemen, that it may be an argument to them to qualify themselves in Parliamentary learning, in such a manner, as that they may rely upon their own abilities, in order to the serving of their Country.

But to come to the point in question; it is not without precedent, that practising lawyers have been excluded from serving in Parliament;[2] and, without following those patterns strictly, I cannot but think it reasonable, that whilst a Parliament sitteth, no Member of Parliament should plead at the bar.

---

[1] *I.e.* the lawyers.

[2] *E.g.* in the Parliament summoned at Coventry in October in 1404 Henry IV. directed that no lawyers should be returned as members. This Parliament was called the 'Unlearned Parliament,' not, the clergy maintained, because of the absence of the lawyers, but because it made a formidable attempt to appropriate the temporalities of the clergy for the financial exigencies of the State. Lawyers had since 1372 been forbidden to serve as knights of the Shire.

The reason of it is in many respects strong in itself, and is grown much stronger by the long sitting of Parliaments of late; but I will not dwell upon this: the matter now in question being concerning lawyers being elected, which I conceive should be done with so much circumspection, that probably it would not often happen.

If lawyers have great practice, that ought to take them up; if not, it is no great sign of their ability; and at the same time giveth a suspicion, that they may be more liable to be tempted.

If it should be so in fact, that no king ever wanted judges to soften the stiffness of the laws that were made, so as to make them suit better with the reason of state, and the convenience of the Government; it is no injury now to suppose it possible for lawyers in the House of Commons, so to behave themselves in the making of new laws, as the better to make way for the having their robes lined with fur.

They are men used to argue on both sides of the question; and if ordinary fees can inspire them with very good reasons in a very ill cause, that faculty exercised in Parliaments, where it may be better encouraged, may prove very inconvenient to those that choose them.

And therefore, without arraigning a possession, that it would be scandalous for a man not to honour; one may, by a suspicion, which is the more excusable when it is in behalf of the people, imagine that the habit of taking money for their opinion, may create in some such a forgetfulness to distinguish, that they may take it for their vote.

They are generally men who by a laborious study hope to be advanced: they have it in their eye as a reward for the toil they undergo.

This maketh them generally very slow, and ill disposed (let the occasion never so much require it) to wrestle with that soil where preferment groweth.

Now if the supposition be in itself not unreasonable, that it should happen to be strengthened and confirmed by experience, it will be very unnecessary to say any more upon this Article, but leave it to the electors to consider of it.

XV. I cannot forbear to put in a caveat against men tied to a Party.

There must in everybody be a leaning to that sort of men who profess some principles, more than to others who go upon a different foundation; but when a man is drowned in a Party, plunged in it beyond his depth, he runneth a great hazard of being upon ill terms with good sense, or morality, if not with both of them.

Such a man can hardly be called a free agent, and for that reason is very unfit to be trusted with the people's liberty, after he hath given up his own.

It is said, that in some part of the *Indies* they do so affect little feet, that they keep them squeezed while they are children, so that they stay at that small size after they are grown men.

One may say something like this of men locked up in a Party; they put their thoughts into such a narrow mould, that they can never be enlarged nor released from their first confinements.

Men in a party have *liberty* only for their *motto*: in reality they are greater slaves than anybody else would care to make them.

A party, even in times of peace, (though against the original contract, and the Bill of Rights) sets up and continues the exercise cise of Martial law; once enrolled, the man that quitteth, if they had their will, would be hanged for a deserter.

They communicate anger to one another by contagion and it may be said, that if too much light dazzleth the eyesight, too much heat doth not less weaken the judgment.

Heat reigneth in the fancy; and reason, which is a colder faculty of the brain, taketh more time to be heard, than the other will allow.

The heat of a party is like the burning of a fever; and not a natural warmth, evenly distributed to give life and vigor.

There was a time indeed when anger shewed a good sign of honesty; but that evidence is very much weakened by instances we have seen since the days of yore: and the public spirited choler hath been thrown off within the time of memory, and lost almost all its credit with some people, since they found what governments thought fit to make their so doing a step to their preferment.

A strong blustering wind seldom continues long in one corner.

Some men knock loud only to be let in; the bustle they make is animated by their private interest. The outward blaze only is for religion and liberty. The true lasting fire, like that of the vestals which never went out, is an eagerness to get somewhat for themselves.

A House of Commons composed of such men, would be more properly so many merchants incorporated in a regular company, to make their particular adventures, than men sent by the people to serve and represent them.

There are some splenetic gentlemen who confine their favourable opinion within so narrow a compass, that they will not allow it to any man that was not hanged in the late reigns.[1]

Now by that rule one might expect they should rescue themselves from the disadvantage of being now alive; and by abdicating a world so little worthy of them, get a great name to themselves, with the general satisfaction of all those they would leave behind them.

Amongst the many ill consequences of a stated party, it is none of the least, that it tempteth low and insignificant men to come upon the stage, to expose themselves, and to spoil business.

It turneth a cypher into a figure, such a one as it is: a man in a party is able to make a noise, let it be never so empty a sound.

[1] *I.e.* the reigns of Charles II. and James II.; the 'splenetic gentlemen' are the Whigs. Halifax himself studiously stood aloof from both parties.

A weak man is easily blown out of his small senses, by being mustered into a Party; he is flattered till he liketh himself so well, that he taketh it extremely ill if he hath not an employment.

Nothing is more in fashion, than for men to desire good places, and I doubt nothing is less so than to deserve them.

From nobody to somebody is such a violent stride, that nature, which hath the negative voice, will not give its royal assent to it: so that when insufficient men aim at being in business, the worst of their enemies might out of malice to them pray for their preferment.

There could be no end, if one did not stop till this theme had no more matter to furnish. I will only say, nothing is more evident, than that the good of the nation hath been sacrificed to the animosities of the several contending parties; and without entering into the dispute which of them are more or less in the right, it is pretty sure, that whilst these opposite sets of angry men are playing at foot-ball, they will break all the windows, and do more hurt than their pretended zeal for the nation will ever make amends for.

In short a man so engaged is retained before

the people take him for their Council; he hath such a reserve for his Party, that it is not advisable for those who choose him, to depend upon his professions. All Parties assuming such a dispensing power, that by their sovereign authority they cancel and dissolve any act or promise that they do not afterwards approve.

These things considered, those who will choose such men deserve whatever followeth.

XVI. Pretenders to exorbitant merit in the late Revolution,[1] are not without objections against them, when they stand to serve in Parliament. It would not only be a low, but a criminal kind of envy, to deny a distinguishing justice to men who have been instrumental and active, when the service of their country required it. But there ought to be moderation in men's claims, or else it is out of the power of our poor island to satisfy them.

It is true, service of all kinds is grown much dearer, like labourer's wages, which formerly occasioned several statutes to regulate them.[2]

But now the men who only carry mortar to

---

[1] Of 1688.

[2] The Statute of Labourers, 1351, attempted to fix wages which had risen after the Black Death; it was followed by many others with a similar purpose, and all were equally futile.

the building, when it is finished, think they are ill dealt with if they are not made master-workmen.

They presently cry out, the original contract is broken, if their merit is not rewarded, at their own rate too.

Some will think there never ought to be an end of their rewards; when indifferent[1] judges would perhaps be puzzled to find out the beginning of their merit.

They bring in such large bills, that they must be examined: some bounds must be put to men's pretensions; else the nation, which is to pay the reckoning, will every way think it a scurvy thing to be undone, whether it be by being over-run by our enemies, or by the being exhausted by our friends.

There ought therefore to be deductions where they are reasonable, the better to justify the paying what remaineth.

For example, if any of these passionate lovers of the Protestant religion, should not think fit, in their manner of living, to give the least evidence of their morality, their claims upon that head might sure be struck off without any injustice to them.

If there are any who set down great sums as

[1] *I.e.* impartial.

a reward due to their zeal for rescuing property from the jaws of arbitrary power; their pretensions may fairly be rejected, if now they are so far from shewing a care and tenderness of the laws, that they look rather like Council retained on the other side.

It is no less strange, than I doubt it is true, that some men should be so in love with their dear mistress, *Old England,* with all her wrinkles, as out of an heroic passion to swim over to rescue her from being ravished; and when they have done the feat, the first thing after enjoyment is, that they go about to strangle her.

For the sake of true love, it is not fit that such ungentle gallants should be too much encouraged; and their arrogance for having done well at first, will have no right to be excused, if their so doing ill at last doth not make them a little more modest.

True merit, like a river, the deeper it is the less noise it makes.

These loud proclaimers of their own deserts, are not only to be suspected for their truth, but the electors are to consider that such meritorious men lay an assessment upon those that choose them.

The public taxes are already heavy enough

without the addition of these private reckonings. It is therefore the safer way not to employ men, who will expect more for their wages than the mistaken Borough that sendeth them up to Parliament could be sold for.

XVII. With all due regard to the noblest of callings, military officers are out of their true element when they are misplaced in a House of Commons.

Things in this world ought to be well suited. There are some appearances so unnatural, that men are convinced by them without any other argument.

The very habit in some cases, recommendeth or giveth offence.

If the judges upon the bench should instead of their furs, which signify gravity and bespeak respect, be cloathed like the jockeys at *Newmarket*, or wear jack-boots and *Steenkirks*; they would not in reality have less law, but mankind would be so struck with this unusual object, that it would be a great while before they could think it possible to receive justice from men so accoutered.

It is to some degree the same thing in this case; such martial habits, Blue-coats, red stockings, &c., make them look very unlike grave senators. One would almost swear they were creatures apart, and of a differing species from the rest of the body.

In former times, when only the resiant shopkeeper was to represent his corporation (which by the way is the law still at this day) the military looks of one of these sons of *Mars* would have stared the quaking Member down again to his Borough.

Now the number of them is so increased, that the peaceable part of the House may lawfully swear they are in fear of their lives, from such an awful appearance of men of war.

It maketh the room look like a Guardhouse by such an ill-suited mixture. But this is only the outside, the bark of the argument; the root goeth yet deeper against choosing such men, whose talents ought to be otherwise applied.

Their two capacities are so inconsistent, that men's undertaking to serve both the cures, will be the cause in a little time that we shall neither have men of war, nor men of business, good in their several kinds.

An officer is to give up his liberty to obey orders; and it is necessary to his calling that he should do so.

A member of Parliament is originally to be tender of his own liberty, that other men may the better trust him with theirs.

An officer is to enable himself by his courage, improved by skill and experience, to support the laws (if invaded) when they are made; but he is not supposed to be at leisure enough to understand how they should be made.

A member of Parliament is to fill his thoughts with what may best conduce to the Civil Administration; which is enough to take up the whole man, let him be never so much raised above the ordinary level.

These two opposite qualifications, being placed in one man, make him such an ambiguous divided creature, that he doth not know how to move.

It is best to keep men within their proper sphere; few men have understanding enough exactly to fill even one narrow circle, fewer are able to fill two; especially when they are both of so great compass and that they are so contrary in their own natures.

The wages he hath as member,[1] and those he

---

[1] Originally the custom of paying members was universal; they were paid by their constituencies, not out of the imperial exchequer, and towns not infrequently petitioned to be relieved of the duty of sending members to Parliament on account of the burden which the necessity of paying them involved; the custom only rested on common law, and was not enforced by statute. As membership of Parliament came to be regarded as an honour, members were found willing to serve without payment,

receiveth as an officer, are paid for services that are very differing; and in the doubt which of them should be preferably performed, it is likely the greater salary may direct him, without the further inducements of complying most, where he may expect most advantage by it.

In short, if his dependance is not very great, it will make him a scurvy officer; if it is great, it will make him a scurvier member.

XVIII. Men under the scandal of being thought private pensioners, are too fair a mark to escape being considered, in reference to the point in question.

In case of plain evidence, it is not to be supposed possible, that men convicted of such a crime should ever again be elected.

The difficulty is in determining what is to be done in case of suspicion.

There are suspicions so well grounded, that they may pretend to have the force of proofs, provided the penalty goeth only to the forbearing to trust, but not extending it so far as to punish.

There must be some things plain and express to justify the latter, but circumstances may be sufficient for the former: as where men have

and the custom became obsolete. Payment is usually considered to have ceased in Elizabeth's reign, but Halifax here implies that it was customary as late as William III.'s reign.

had such sudden cures of their ill humours, and opposition to the Court, that it is out of the way of ordinary methods of recovery from such distemper, which have a much slower progress; it must naturally be imputed to some specific that maketh such a quick alteration of the whole mass of blood.[1]

Where men have raised their way of living, without any visible means to support them in it, a suspicion is justified, even by the example of the law, which in cases of this kind, though of an inferior nature, doth upon this foundation not only raise inferences, but inflict punishments.

Where men are immoral, and scandalous in their lives, and dispense familiarly with the rules by which the world is governed, for the better preserving the bonds of human society; it must be a confidence very ill placed, to conclude it impossible for such men to yield to a temptation well offered and pursued; when, the truth is, the habit of such *Bons vivants*,

---

[1] The difficulty of dealing with 'placemen,' or those who held pensions or offices at Court, of which much is heard during the eighteenth century, was not satisfactorily settled until Rockingham's Act of 1782. The acceptance of a place of profit under the Crown still vacates a member's seat: indeed, two of these nominal places of profit, the stewardship of the Chiltern Hundreds and Northstead Manor afford the only means of enabling a member to resign his seat.

which is the fashionable word, maketh a suspicion so likely, that it is very hard not to believe it to be true.

If there should be nothing but the general report, even that is not to be neglected.

Common fame is the only liar that deserveth to have some respect still reserved to it; though she telleth many an untruth, she often hits right, and most especially when she speaketh ill of men.

Her credit hath sometimes been carried too far, when it hath gone to the divesting men of any thing of which they were possessed, without more express evidence to justify such a proceeding.

If there was a doubt whether there ever was any corruption of this kind it would alter the question; but sure that will not bear the being controverted.

We are told, that Charles the fifth sent over to England 1,200,000 crowns [1] to be distributed amongst the leading men, to encourage them to carry on elections.

Here was the Protestant religion to be bought out for a valuable consideration accord-

---

[1] Apparently the bullion estimated at £50,000, which Philip brought over with him on his marriage to Mary in 1554.

ing to law, though not according to Gospel, which exalteth it above any price that can be set on it.

Now, except we had reason to believe that the virtue of the world is improved since that time, we can as little doubt that such temptations may be offered, as that they will be received.

It will be owned, that there is to be a great tenderness in suspecting; but it must be allowed at the same time, that there ought not to be less in trusting, where the people are so much concerned; especially, when the penalty on the party suspected goeth no further than a suspension of that confidence, which it is necessary to have in those who are to represent the nation in Parliament.

I cannot omit the giving a caution against admitting men to be chosen, who have places of any value.

There needeth the less to be said on this article, the truth of the proposition being supported by such plain arguments.

Sure no man hath such a plentiful spring of thought as that all that floweth from it is too much to be applied to the business of Parliament.

It is not less sure, that a Member of Parliament, of all others, ought not to be exempted from the rule, that no man should serve two masters.

It doth so split a man's thoughts, that no man can know how to make a fitting distribution of them to two such differing capacities.

It exposeth men to be suspected, and tempted, more than is convenient for the public service, or for the mutual good opinion of one another, which there ought to be in such an assembly.

It either giveth a real dependance upon the Government, which is inconsistent with the necessity there is, that a member of Parliament should be disengaged; or at least it hath the appearance of it, which maketh them not look like freemen, though they should have virtue enough to be so.

More reasons would lessen the weight of this last, which is, that a bill to this effect commonly called the *Self Denying Bill*, passed even this last House of Commons.[1]

---

[1] *I.e.* the Place Bill, providing that no member should accept any place of profit under the Crown on pain of forfeiting his seat and being incapable of sitting again in the same parliament, passed the Commons in 1693. The Lords inserted the clause 'unless he be afterwards again chosen to serve in the same parliament,' to which the Commons agreed. The king, however, vetoed it, and when it was re-introduced in 1694 it failed to pass the Commons.—See Macaulay, ii. 4734, 497.

A greater demonstration of the irresistible strength of truth cannot possibly be given; so that a copy of that Bill in every County or Borough, would hardly fail of discouraging such pretenders from standing, or at least it would prevent their success if their own modesty should not restrain them from attempting it.

XX. If distinctions may be made upon particular men, or remarks fixed upon their votes in Parliament, they must be allowed in relation to those gentlemen, who for reasons best known to themselves thought fit to be against the *Triennial Bill*.[1]

The liberty of opinion is the thing in the world that ought least to be controlled, and especially in Parliament.

But as that is an undoubted assertion, it is not less so, that when men sin against their own light, give a vote against their own thought, they must not plead privilege of Parliament against being arraigned for it by others, after they are convicted of it by themselves.

There cannot be a man, who in his definition of a House of Commons, will state it to be

---

[1] Passed in 1694: there was little opposition to it then, but in the previous session it had been unexpectedly defeated in the Commons.—Macaulay, ii. 473.

an assembly, that for the better redressing of grievances the People feel, and for the better furnishing such supplies as they can bear, is to continue, if the King so pleaseth for his whole reign.

This could be as little intended, as to throw all into one hand, and to renounce the claim to any liberty, but so much as the sovereign authority would allow.

It destroyeth the end of Parliaments, it maketh use of the letter of the law to extinguish the life of it.

It is, in truth, some kind of disparagement to so plain a thing, that so much has been said and written upon it; and one may say, it is such an affront to these gentlemen's understandings to censure this vote only as a mistake, that, as the Age goeth, it is less discredit to them to call it by its right name; and if that is rightly understood by those who are to choose them, I suppose they will let them exercise their liberty of conscience at home, and not make men their trustees, who in this solemn instance have such an unwillingness to surrender.

It must be owned, that this Bill hath met with very hard fortune, and yet that doth not in the least diminish the value of it.

It had in it such a root of life, that it might be said, it was not dead but sleeped; and we see that the last session, it was revived and animated by the royal assent, when once fully informed of the consequence, as well as of the justice of it.

In the mean time, after having told my opinion, who ought not to be chosen:

If I should be asked, who ought to be, my answer must be, choose *Englishmen;* and when I have said that, to deal honestly, I will not undertake that they are easy to be found.[1]

---

[1] A parting shot at the number of William III. Dutch favourites.

IV

THE ART OF POLITICAL LYING

[This pamphlet was written in 1712 by John Arbuthnot (1667-1735), the doctor and wit of Queen Anne's time and the friend of Swift, Pope, and Gay. It has frequently been attributed to Swift, and Scott printed it in his edition of Swift's works; it is possible that Swift had a hand in it, but Swift himself[1] says that Arbuthnot wrote it. It is one of the most delightful pieces of ironical writing in the language, and there are not wanting those who maintain that it is as much *à propos* of politics to-day as it was nearly two centuries ago.]

THERE is now in the press, a curious piece, entitled ψευδολογία πολιτική; or, The Art of Political Lying: consisting of two volumes in quarto. The proposals are, i. That, if the author meets with suitable encouragement, he intends to deliver the first volume to the subscribers by Hilary Term next. ii. The price of both volumes will be, to the subscribers, fourteen shillings, seven whereof are to be paid down, and the other seven at the delivery of

[1] Journal to Stella. 12 Dec. 1712.

the second volume. iii. Those that subscribe for six, shall have a seventh *gratis;* which reduces the price to less than six shillings a volume. iv. That the subscribers shall have their names and places of abode printed at length. For the encouragement of so useful a work, it is thought fit the public should be informed of the contents of the first volume, by one who has with great care perused the manuscript.

THE ART OF POLITICAL LYING.

The author, in his preface, makes some very judicious reflections upon the original of arts and sciences: that at first they consist of scattered theorems and practices, which are handed about among the masters, and only revealed to the *filii artis,* till such time as some great genius appears, who collects these disjointed propositions, and reduces them into a regular system. That is the case of that noble and useful art of Political Lying, which in this last age having been enriched with several new discoveries, ought not to lie any longer in rubbish and confusion, but may justly claim a place in the Encyclopædia, especially such as serves for a model of education for an able politician. That he proposes to himself no small stock of fame in future ages, in being the first who has undertaken this design; and for the same reason he hopes the imperfection of his work will be excused. He invites all persons who have any talents that way, or any new discovery, to communicate their thoughts, assuring them that honourable mention shall be made of them in his work.

The first Volume consists of Eleven Chapters.

In the first chapter of his excellent treatise, he reasons philosophically concerning the nature of the soul of man, and those qualities which render it susceptible of lies. He supposes the soul to be of the nature of a plano-cylindrical speculum, or looking-glass; that the plain side was made by God Almighty, but that the devil afterwards wrought the other into a cylindrical figure. The plain side represents objects just as they are; and the cylindrical side, by the rules of catoptrics, must needs represent true objects false, and false objects true; but the cylindrical side being much the larger surface, takes in a greater compass of visual rays. That upon the cylindrical side of the soul of man depends the whole art and success of political lying. The author, in this chapter, proceeds to reason upon the qualities of the mind: as its peculiar fondness of the malicious and miraculous. The tendency of the soul toward the malicious, springs from self-love, or a pleasure to find mankind more wicked, base, or unfortunate, than ourselves. The design of the miraculous proceeds from the inactivity of the soul, or its incapacity to be moved or delighted with anything that is vulgar or common. The author having established the qualities of the mind, upon which his art is founded, he proceeds,

In his second chapter, to treat of the nature of political lying; which he defines to be, 'the art of convincing the people of salutary falsehoods, for some good end.' He calls it an art to distinguish it from that of telling truth, which does not seem to want art; but then he would have this understood only as to the invention, because there is indeed more art necessary to convince the people of a salutary truth, than a salutary falsehood. Then he proceeds to prove, that there are salutary falsehoods, of which he gives a great many instances, both before and after the Revolution; and demonstrates plainly, that we could not have carried on the war so long without several of those salutary falsehoods. He gives

THE ART OF POLITICAL LYING

rules to calculate the value of a political lie, in pounds, shillings, and pence. By good, he does not mean that which is absolutely so, but what appears so to the artist, which is a sufficient ground for him to proceed upon; and he distinguishes the good, as it commonly is, into *bonum utile, dulce, et honestum*. He shows you that there are political lies of a mixed nature, which include all the three in different respects; that the *utile* reigns generally about the Exchange, the *dulce* and *honestum* at the Westminster end of the town. One man spreads a lie to sell or buy stock to greater advantage; a second, because it is honourable to serve his party; and a third, because it is sweet to gratify his revenge. Having explained the several terms of his definition, he proceeds,

In his third chapter, to treat of the lawfulness of political lying; which he deduces from its true and genuine principles, by inquiring into the several rights, that mankind have to truth. He shews that people have a right to private truth from their neighbours, and economical truth from their own family; that they should not be abused by their wives, children, and servants; but that they have no right at all to political truth; that the people may as well all pretend to be lords of manors, and possess great estates, as to have truth told them in matters of government. The author, with great judgment, states the several shares of mankind in this matter of truth, according to their several capacities, dignities, and professions; and shews you that children have hardly any share at all; in consequence of which, they have very seldom any truth told them. It must be owned, that the author, in this chapter, has some seeming difficulties to answer, and texts of Scripture to explain.

The fourth chapter is wholly employed in this question, "Whether the right of coinage of political lies be wholly in the government?" The author, who is a true friend to English liberty, determines in the negative, and answers all the arguments of the opposite party with great acuteness: that as the government of England has a mixture of democratical in it, so the right of inventing and spreading political lies is partly in the people; and their obstinate adherence to this just privilege has been most conspicuous, and shined with great lustre of late years: that it happens very often, that there are no other means left to the good people of England to pull down a ministry and government they are weary of, but by exercising this their undoubted right: that abundance of political lying is a sure sign of true English liberty: that as ministers do sometimes use tools to support their power, it is but reasonable that the people should employ the same weapon to defend themselves, and pull them down.

In his fifth chapter, he divides political lies into several species and classes, and gives precepts about the inventing, spreading, and propagating the several sorts of them: he begins with the *rumores* and *libelli famosi*, such as concern the reputation of men in power; where he finds fault with the common mistake, that takes notice only of one sort, viz. the detractory or defamatory; whereas in truth there are three sorts, the detractory, the additory, and the translatory. The additory gives to a great man a larger share of reputation than belongs to him, to enable him to serve some good end or purpose. The detractory, or defamatory, is a lie which takes from a great man the reputation that justly belongs to him, for fear he should use it to the detriment of the public. The translatory is a lie, that transfers the merit of a man's good action to another, who is in himself more deserving; or transfers the demerit of a bad action from the true author to a person who is in himself less deserving. He gives several instances of very great strokes in all the three kinds, especially in the last, when it was necessary for the good of the public, to bestow the valour and conduct of one man upon another, and that of many to one man: nay even, upon a good occasion, a man may be robbed of his victory by a person that did not command in the action.[1] The restoring and destroying the public may be ascribed to persons who had no hand in either. The author exhorts all gentlemen practitioners to exercise themselves in the translatory, because the existence of the things themselves being visible, and not demanding any proof, there wants nothing to be put upon the public, but a false author, or a false cause; which is no great presumption upon the credulity of mankind, to whom the secret springs of things are for the most part unknown.

The author proceeds to give some precepts as to the additory; that when one ascribes anything to a person which does not belong to him, the lie ought to be calculated not quite

---

[1] Probably an allusion to General Webb's success at Wynendal on 28 Sept. 1708. Webb's name was accidentally omitted in the gazette that described the action. The Tories raised a great outcry over the matter, imputing the omission to Marlborough's jealousy.

contradictory to his known qualities; for example one would not make the French King present at a Protestant conventicle; nor, like Queen Elizabeth, restore the overplus of taxes to his subjects. One would not bring in the Emperor giving two months' pay in advance to his troops; nor the Dutch paying more than their quota. One would not make the same person zealous for a standing army, and public liberty;[1] nor an atheist support the church, nor a lewd fellow a reformer of manners; nor a hot-headed, crack-brained coxcomb forward for a scheme of moderation. But, if it is absolutely necessary that a person is to have some good adventitious quality given him, the author's precept is, that it should not be done at first *in extremo gradu*. For example, they should not make a covetous man give away all at once five thousand pounds in a charitable, generous way; twenty or thirty pounds may suffice at first. They should not introduce a person of remarkable ingratitude to his benefactors, rewarding a poor man for some good office that was done him thirty years ago; but they may allow him to acknowledge a service

[1] A standing army was then thought to be incompatible with public liberty, an idea fostered by Cromwell's rule and James II.'s endeavours to use the army to render himself absolute.

to a person, who is capable still to do him another. A man, whose personal courage is suspected, is not at first to drive whole squadrons before him, but he may be allowed the merit of some squabble, or throwing a bottle at his adversary's head.

It will not be allowed to make a great man, that is a known despiser of religion, spend whole days in his closet at his devotion; but you may with safety make him sit out public prayers with decency. A great man, who has never been known willingly to pay a just debt, ought not all of a sudden, to be introduced making restitutions of thousands he has cheated; let it suffice at first to pay twenty pounds to a friend, who has lost his note.

He lays down the same rules in the detractory or defamatory kind; that they should not be quite opposite to the qualities the persons are supposed to have. Thus it will not be found according to the sound rules of pseudology, to report of a pious and religious Prince, that he neglects his devotion, and would introduce heresy; but you may report of a merciful Prince, that he has pardoned a criminal, who did not deserve it. You will be unsuccessful if you give out of a great man, who is remarkable for his frugality for the public, that he squanders away the nation's money; but you may safely relate that he hoards it: you must not affirm he took a bribe, but you may freely censure him for being tardy in his payments; because, though neither may be true, yet the last is credible, the first not. Of an openhearted, generous minister, you are not to say, that he was in an intrigue to betray his country; but you may affirm, with some probability, that he was in an intrigue with a lady. He warns all practitioners to take good heed to these precepts; for want of which, many of their lies of late have proved abortive or short-lived.

In the sixth chapter, he treats of the miraculous; by which he understands anything that exceeds the common degrees of probability. In respect to the people, it is divided into two sorts, the τὸ φοβερὸν or the τὸ θυμοειδες, terrifying lies, and animating or encouraging lies; both being extremely useful on their proper occasions. Concerning the τὸ φοβερὸν, he gives several rules; one of which is, that terrible objects should not be too frequently shewn to the people, lest they grow familiar. He says, it is absolutely necessary that the people of England should be frighted with the French King and the Pretender once a-year; but that the bears should be chained up again till that time twelvemonth. The want of observing this so necessary a precept, in bringing out the raw head and bloody bones upon every trifling occasion, has produced great indifference in the vulgar of late years. As to the animating or encouraging lies, he gives the following rules that they shall not far exceed the common degrees of probability; that there should be variety of them; and the same lie not obstinately insisted upon: that the promissory or prognosticating lies should not be on short days, for fear the authors should have the shame and confusion to see themselves speedily contradicted. He examines, by these rules, that well-meant but unfortunate lie of the conquest of France which continued near twenty years together; but at last, by being too obstinately insisted upon, it was worn threadbare, and became unsuccessful.

As to the τὸ τερατῶδες, or the prodigious, he has little to advise, but that their comets, whales, and dragons should be sizeable; their storms, tempests, and earth quakes without the reach of a day's journey of a man and horse.

The seventh chapter is wholly taken up in an inquiry, which of the two parties are the greatest artists in political lying. He owns, that sometimes the one party, and sometimes the other is better believed; but that they have both very good geniuses among them. He attributes the ill success of either party to their glutting the market, and retailing too much of a bad commodity at once: when there is too great a quantity of worms, it is hard to catch gudgeons. He proposes a scheme for the recovery of the credit of any party, which indeed seems to be somewhat chimerical, and does not savour of that sound judgment the author has shewn in the rest of the work. It amounts to this, that the party should agree to vent nothing but truth for three months together, which will give them credit for six months lying afterwards. He owns, that he believes it almost impossible to find fit persons to execute this scheme. Towards the end of the chapter, he inveighs severely against the folly of parties retaining scoundrels, and men of low genius, to retail their lies; such as most of the present news-writers are; who, except a strong bent and inclination towards the profession, seem to be wholly ignorant in the rules of pseudology, and not at all qualified for so weighty a trust.

In his next chapter, he treats of some extraordinary geniuses, who have appeared of late years, especially in their disposition towards the miraculous. He advises those hopeful young men to turn their invention to the service of their country; it being inglorious, at this time, to employ their talent in prodigious fox-chases, horse-courses, feats of activity in driving of coaches, jumping, running, swallowing of peaches, pulling out whole sets of teeth to clean, etc., when their country stands in so much need of their assistance.

The eighth chapter is a project for uniting the several smaller corporation of liars into one society. It is too tedious to give a full account of the whole scheme: what is most remarkable is, that this society ought to consist of the heads of each party; that no lie is to pass current without their approbation, they being the best judges of the present exigences, and what sorts of lies are demanded; that in such a corporation there ought to be men of all professions, that τὸ πρέπον, and the τὸ εὐλόγον, that is, decency and probability, may be observed as much as possible; that, besides the persons above mentioned, this society ought to consist of the hopeful geniuses about the town (of which there are great plenty to be picked up in the several coffee houses,) travellers, virtuosoes, fox-hunters, jockeys, attorneys, old seamen and soldiers out of the hospitals of Greenwich and Chelsea; to this society so constituted, ought to be committed the sole management of lying; that in their outer-room there ought always to attend some persons endowed with a great stock of credulity, a generation that thrives mightily in this soil and climate: he thinks a sufficient number of them may be picked up anywhere about the Exchange: these are to circulate what the others coin; for no man spreads a lie with so good a grace as he that believes it: that the rule of the society be, to invent a lie, and sometimes two for every day; in the choice of which, great regard ought to be had to the weather, and the season of the year: your $\phi o \beta \epsilon \rho \grave{a}$, or terrifying lies, do mighty well in November and December, but not so well in May and June, unless the easterly winds reign: that it ought to be penal for anybody to talk of anything but the lie of the day: that the Society is to maintain a sufficient number of spies at Court, and other places, to furnish hints and topics for invention, and a general correspondence of all the market-towns for circulating their lies: that if anyone of the society were observed to blush, or look out of countenance, or want a necessary circumstance in telling the lie, he ought to be expelled, and declared incapable: besides the soaring lies, there ought to be a private committee for whisperers, constituted of the ablest men of the society. Here the author makes a digression in praise of the Whig party, for the right understanding and use of proof-lies. A proof-lie is like a proof-charge for a piece of ordnance, to try a standard credulity. Of such a nature he takes transubstantiation to be in the Church of Rome, a proof article, which if anyone swallows, they are sure he will digest everything else; therefore the Whig party do wisely, to try the credulity of the people sometimes by swingers, that they may be able to judge to what height they may charge them afterwards. Towards the end of this chapter, he warns the heads of parties against believing their own lies, which has proved of pernicious consequences of late; both a wise party, and a wise nation having regulated their affairs upon lies of their own invention. The causes of this he supposes to be, too great a zeal and intenseness in the practice of this art, and a vehement heat in mutual conversation, whereby they persuade one another, that what they wish, and report to be true, is really so: that all parties have been subject to this misfortune. The Jacobites have been constantly infested with it; but the Whigs of late seemed even to exceed them in this ill habit and weakness. To this chapter the author subjoins a calendar of lies proper for the several months of the year.

The ninth chapter treats of the celerity and duration of lies. As to the celerity of their motion, the author says it is almost incredible: he gives several instances of lies, that have gone faster than a man can ride post: your terrifying lies travel at a prodigious rate, above ten miles an hour: your whispers move in a narrow vortex, but very swiftly. The author says, it is impossible to explain several phenomena in relation to the celerity of lies, without the supposition of synchronism and combination. As to the duration of lies, he says there are of all sorts, from hours and days, to ages; that there are some, which, like insects, die and revive again in a different form; that good artists, like people who build upon a short lease, will calculate the duration of a lie surely to answer their purpose; to last just as long, and no longer, than the turn is served.

The tenth chapter treats of the characteristics of lies; how to know when, where, and by whom, invented. Your Dutch, English, and French ware are amply distinguished from one another; an Exchange lie from one coined at the other end of the town: great judgment is to be shewn as to the place where the species is intended to circulate: very low and base coin will serve for Wapping: there are several coffee-houses, that have their particular stamps, which a judicious practitioner may easily know. All your great men have their proper phantateustics. The author, says he, has attained, by study and application, to so great a skill in this matter, that, bring him any lie, he can tell whose image it bears so truly, as the great man himself shall not have the face to deny it. The promissory lies of great men are known by shouldering, hugging, squeezing, smiling, bowing; and their lies in matter of fact, by immoderate swearing.

He spends the whole eleventh chapter on one simple question, Whether a lie is best contradicted by truth, or by another lie? The author, says, that considering the large extent of the cylindrical surface of the soul, and the great propensity to believe lies in the generality of mankind of late years, he thinks the properest contradiction to a lie, is another lie. For example; if it should be reported that the Pretender was at London, one would not contradict it by saying, he never was in England; but you must prove by eyewitnesses, that he came no farther than Greenwich, and then went back again. Thus if it be spread about, that a great person were dying of some disease, you must not say the truth, that they are in health and never had such a disease, but that they are slowly recovering of it. So there was not long ago a gentleman, who affirmed, that the treaty with France, for bringing popery and slavery into England, was signed the 15th of September; to which another answered very judiciously, not, by opposing truth to his lie, that there was no such treaty; but that, to his certain knowledge, there were many things in that treaty not yet adjusted.

[The account of the second volume of this excellent treatise is reserved for another time.]

V

THE CRISIS

[This famous pamphlet was written by Richard Steele in 1713, and on 18 March 1714 he was expelled from the House of Commons, ostensibly because he had written this pamphlet, really because of his pronounced Whig views. The object of the pamphlet was to show the dangers of the Pretender succeeding to the throne, both to the Protestant religion and political liberty. Steele knew that a serious attempt was preparing to overthrow the Act of Succession. He addresses the 'Crisis' to the clergy of the church of England, who were, as Swift said, almost Tory to a man. But though Tory they hated Roman Catholicism and the Pretender was known to be a bigoted Catholic: thus though they had no love for the house of Hanover they dreaded still more the advent of a Roman Catholic prince.]

TO THE

CLERGY OF THE CHURCH OF ENGLAND.

GENTLEMEN,

It is with a just deference to your great power and influence in this kingdom, that I lay before you the following comment upon the laws which regard the settlement of the Imperial Crown of Great Britain. My purpose in addressing these matters to you, is to conjure you, as Heaven has blessed you with proper talents and opportunities, to recommend them, in your writings and discourses, to your fellow-subjects.

In the character of pastors and teachers, you have an almost irresistible power over us of your congregations; and by the admirable institution of our laws, the tenths of our lands, now in your possession, are destined to become the property of such others as shall by learning and virtue qualify themselves to succeed you. These circumstances of education and fortune place the minds of the people, from age to age, under your direction. As, therefore, it would be the highest indiscretion in Ministers of State of this kingdom to neglect the care of being acceptable to you in their administration, so it would be the greatest impiety in you to inflame the people committed to your charge with apprehensions of danger to you and your constitution, from men innocent of any such designs.

Give me leave, who have in all my words and actions, from my youth upwards, maintained an inviolable respect to you and your order, to observe to you that all the dissatisfactions which have been raised in the minds of the people owe their rise to the cunning of artful men, who have introduced the mention of you and your interest, which are sacred to all good men, to cover and sanctify their own practices upon the affections of the people, for ends very different from the promotion of religion and virtue. Give me leave also to take notice that these suggestions have been favoured by some few unwary men in holy orders, who have made the constitution of their own country a very little part of their study, and yet made obedience and government the frequent subjects of their discourses.

These men, from the pompous ideas of imperial greatness, and submission to absolute emperors, which they imbibed in their earlier years, have from time to time inadvertently uttered notions of power and obedience abhorrent from the laws of this their native country.

I will take the further liberty to say, that if the Acts of Parliament mentioned in the following treatise had been from time to time put in a fair and clear light, and been carefully recommended to the perusal of young gentlemen in colleges, with a preference to all other civil institutions whatsoever, this kingdom had not been in its present condition, but the constitution would have had, in every member the universities have sent into the world ever since the Revolution, an advocate for our rights and liberties.

There is one thing which deserves your most serious consideration. You have bound yourselves, by the strongest engagements that religion can lay upon men, to support that succession which is the subject of the following papers; you have tied down your souls by an oath to maintain it as it is settled in the House of Hanover; nay, you have gone much further than is usual in cases of this nature, as you have personally abjured the Pretender to this Crown, and that expressly, without any equivocations or mental reservations whatsoever, that is, without any possible escapes, by which the subtlety of temporizing casuists might hope to elude the force of these solemn obligations. You know much better than I do, whether the calling God to witness to the sincerity of our intentions in these cases, whether the swearing upon the holy Evangelists in the most solemn manner, whether the taking of an oath before multitudes of fellow-subjects and fellow-Christians in our public courts of justice, do not lay the greatest obligations that can be laid on the consciences of men. This I am sure of, that if the body of a clergy who considerately and voluntarily entered into these engagements should be made use of as instruments and examples to make the nation break through them, not only the succession to our Crown, but the very essence of our religion, is in danger. What a triumph would it furnish to those evil men among us who are enemies to your sacred order? What occasion would it administer to atheists and unbelievers, to say that Christianity is nothing else but an outward show and pretence among the most knowing of its professors? What could we afterwards object to Jesuits? What would be the scandal brought upon our holy Church, which is at present the glory and bulwark of the Reformation? How would our present clergy appear in the eyes of their posterity, and even to the successors of their own order, under a Government introduced and established by a conduct so directly opposite to all the rules of honour and precepts of Christianity?

As I always speak and think of your holy

order with the utmost deference and respect, I do not insist upon this subject to insinuate that there is such a disposition among your venerable body, but to show how much your own honour and the interest of religion is concerned that there should be no cause given for it.

Under colour of a zeal towards you, men may sometimes act not only with impunity, but popularity, what would render them, without that hypocrisy, insufferably odious to their fellow-subjects.

Under this pretence men may presume to practise such arts for the destruction and dishonour of their country as it would be impious to make use of even for its glory and safety; men may do in the highest prosperity what it would not be excusable to attempt under the lowest necessity!

The laws of our country, the powers of the legislature, the faith of nations, and the honour of God may be too weak considerations to bear up against the popular though groundless cry of the Church. This fatal prepossession may shelter men in raising the French name and Roman Catholic interest in Great Britain, and consequently in all Europe.

It behoves you therefore, gentlemen, to consider whether the cry of the Church's danger may not at length become a truth ; and, as you are men of sense and men of honour, to exert yourselves in undeceiving the multitude, whenever their affectionate concern for you may prove fatal to themselves.

You are surrounded by a learned, wealthy, and knowing gentry, who can distinguish your merit, and do honour to your characters. They know with what firmness as Englishmen, with what self-denial as prelates, with what charity as Christians, the Lords the Bishops, fathers of the Church, have behaved themselves in the public cause; they know what contumelies the rest of the clergy have undergone, what discountenance they have laboured under, what prejudice they have suffered in their ministry, who have adhered to the cause of truth; but it is certain that the face of things is now too melancholy to bear any longer false appearances; and common danger has united men, who not long ago were artfully inflamed against each other, into some regard of their common safety.

When the world is in this temper, those of our pastors, whose exemplary lives and charitable dispositions both adorn and advance our holy religion, will be the objects of our love and admiration; and those who pursue the gratifications of pride, ambition and avarice, under the sacred character of clergymen, will not fail to be our contempt and derision.

Noise and wrath cannot always pass for zeal; and if we see but little of the public spirit of Englishmen or the charity of Christians in others, it is certain we can feel but little of the pleasure of love and gratitude, and but faint emotions of respect and veneration in ourselves.

It will be an action worthy the ministers of the Church of England to distinguish themselves for the love of their country; and, as we have a religion that wants no assistance from artifice or enlargement of secular power, but is well supported by the wisdom and piety of its preachers, and its own native truth, to let mankind see that we have a clergy who are of the people, obedient to the same laws, and zealous not only of the supremacy and prerogative of our princes, but of the liberties of their fellow-subjects: this will make us who are your flock burn with joy to see, and with zeal to imitate, your lives and actions. It cannot be expected but that there will be, in so great a body, light, superficial, vain, and ambitious men, who, being untouched with the sublime force of the Gospel, will think it their interest to insinuate jealousies between the clergy and laity, in hopes to derive from their order a veneration which they know they cannot deserve from their virtue. But while the most worthy, conspicuous, learned, and powerful of your sacred function are moved by the noble and generous incentives of doing good to the souls of men, we will not doubt of seeing by your ministry the love of our country, due regard for our laws and liberties, and resentment for the abuse of truth revive in the hearts of men. And as there are no instruments under heaven so capable of this great work, that God would make you such to this divided nation is the hearty prayer of,

    Gentlemen,
     Your most dutiful and most obedient humble servant,
       RICHARD STEELE.

VI

SOME FREE THOUGHTS UPON THE PRESENT STATE OF AFFAIRS

[This tract was written by Swift in 1714; he had come over from Ireland in order to reconcile the differences between Harley and Bolingbroke and to persuade his party to reconcile itself to the Elector of Hanover. Himself no Jacobite he had little sympathy with, and apparently no knowledge of, the Jacobite intrigues of Bolingbroke and his followers. Probably for this reason he failed in his attempt, retired to Berkshire, where he wrote this pamphlet. It should be read in connection with Steele's 'Crisis' on the one side and Bolingbroke's 'State of Parties' on the other.]

WHATEVER may be thought or practised by profound politicians, they will hardly be able to convince the reasonable part of mankind, that the most plain, short, easy, safe, and lawful way to any good end, is not more eligible, than one directly contrary to some or all of these qualities. I have been frequently assured by great ministers, that politics were nothing but common sense; which, as it was the only true thing they spoke, so it was the only thing they could have wished I should not believe. God has given the bulk of mankind a capacity to understand reason, when it is fairly offered; and by reason they would easily be governed, if it were left to their choice. Those princes in all ages, who were most distinguished for their mysterious skill in government, found by the event, that they had ill consulted their own quiet, or the ease and happiness of their people; nor has posterity remembered them with honour: such as Lysander and Philip among the Greeks, Tiberius in Rome, Pope Alexander the Sixth and his son Cæsar Borgia, Queen Catherine de Medicis, Philip the Second of Spain, with many others. Nor are examples less frequent of ministers, famed for men of great intrigue, whose politics have produced little more than murmurings, factions, and discontents, which usually terminated in the disgrace and ruin of the authors.

I can recollect but three occasions in a state, where the talents of such men may be thought necessary; I mean in a state where the prince is obeyed and loved by his subjects: first, in the negotiation of the peace; secondly, in adjusting the interests of our own country, with those of the nations round us, watching the several motions of our neighbours and allies, and preserving a due balance among them: lastly, in the management of parties and factions at home. In the first of these cases I have often heard it observed, that plain good sense, and a firm adherence to the point, have proved more effectual than all those arts, which I remember a great foreign minister used in contempt to call the spirit of negotiating. In the second case, much wisdom, and a thorough knowledge of affairs both foreign and domestic, are certainly required: after which, I know no talents necessary beside method and skill in the common forms of business. In the last case, which is that of managing parties, there seems indeed to be more occasion for employing this gift of the lower politics, whenever the tide runs high against the court and ministry; which seldom happens under any tolerable administration, while the true interest of the nation is pursued. But, here in England, (for I do not pretend to establish maxims of government in general,) while the prince and ministry, the clergy, the majority of landed men, and the bulk of the people, appear to have the same views and the same principles, it is not obvious to me, how those at the helm can have many opportunities of showing their skill in mystery and refinement, beside what themselves think fit to create.

I have been assured by men long practised in business, that the secrets of court are much fewer than we generally suppose; and I hold it for the greatest secret of the court, that they are so: because the first springs of great events, like those of rivers, are so often mean and so little, that in decency they ought to be hid: and therefore ministers are so wise to leave their proceedings to be accounted for by reasoners at a distance, who often mould them into systems, that do not only go down very well in the coffeehouse, but are supplies for pamphlets in the present age, and may probably furnish materials for memoirs and histories in the next.

It is true, indeed, that even those who are very near the court, and are supposed to have a large share in the management of public matters, are apt to deduce wrong consequences, by reasoning upon the causes and motives of those actions, wherein themselves are employed. A great minister puts you a case, and asks your opinion, but conceals an essential circumstance, upon which the whole weight of the matter turns; then he despises your understanding for counselling him no better,

and concludes he ought to trust entirely to
his own wisdom. Thus he grows to abound
in secrets and reserves, even towards those
with whom he ought to act in the greatest
confidence and concert: and thus the world
is brought to judge, that whatever be the
issue and event, it was all foreseen, contrived,
and brought to pass by some masterstroke of
his politics.

I could produce innumerable instances, from
my own memory and observation, of events
imputed to the profound skill and address
of a minister,[1] which in reality were either
the mere effects of negligence, weakness,
humour, passion, or pride; or, at best, but
the natural course of things left to themselves.

During this very session of parliament, a
most ingenious gentleman, who has much
credit with those in power, would needs have
it, that, in the late dissensions at court,[2] which
grew too high to be any longer a secret, the
whole matter was carried with the utmost
dexterity on one side, and with manifest ill
conduct on the other. To prove this, he made
use of the most plausible topics, drawn from

---

[1] Probably a reference to Robert Harley, Lord Oxford, who was practically prime minister from 1710 till Bolingbroke procured his dismissal on 27 July 1714.

[2] *I.e.* between Oxford and Bolingbroke.

the nature and disposition of the several persons concerned, as well as of her majesty; all which he knows as much of as any man: and gave me a detail of the whole with such an appearance of probability, as, committed to writing, would pass for an admirable piece of secret history. Yet I am at the same time convinced by the strongest reasons, that the issue of those dissensions, as to the part they had in the court and the House of Lords, was partly owing to very different causes, and partly to the situation of affairs, whence, in that conjuncture, they could not easily terminate otherwise than they did, whatever unhappy consequences they may have for the future.

In like manner, I have heard a physician pronounce with great gravity, that he had cured so many patients of malignant fevers, and as many more of the small-pox; whereas, in truth, nine parts in ten of those who recovered owed their lives to the strength of nature and a good constitution, while such a one happened to be their doctor.

But, while it is so difficult to learn the springs and motives of some facts, and so easy to forget the circumstances of others, it is no wonder they should be so grossly misrepresented to the public by curious inquisitive heads, who proceed altogether upon conjectures, and, in reasoning upon affairs of state, are sure to be mistaken by searching too deep. And as I have known this to be the frequent error of many others, so I am sure it has been perpetually mine, whenever I have attempted to discover the causes of political events by refinement and conjecture; which, I must acknowledge, has very much abated my veneration for what they call *arcana imperii;* whereof I dare pronounce, that the fewer there are in any administration, it is just so much the better.

What I have hitherto said has by no means been intended to detract from the qualities requisite in those who are trusted with the administration of public affairs; on the contrary, I know no station of life, where great abilities and virtues of all kinds are so highly necessary, and where the want of any is so quickly or universally felt. A great minister has no virtue, for which the public may not be the better; nor any defect, by which the public is not certainly a sufferer. I have known more than once or twice within four years past, an omission, in appearance very small, prove almost fatal to a whole scheme, and very hardly retrieved. It is not always sufficient for the person at the helm that he is intrepid in his nature, free from any tincture of avarice or corruption, and that he has great natural and acquired abilities.

I never thought the reputation of much secrecy was a character of any advantage to a minister, because it put all other men upon their guard to be as secret as he, and was consequently the occasion that persons and things were always misrepresented to him: because likewise too great an affectation of secrecy is usually thought to be attended with those little intrigues and refinements, which, among the vulgar, denominate a man a great politician; but among others, is apt, whether deservedly or not, to acquire the opinion of cunning: a talent, which differs as much from the true knowledge of government, as that of an attorney from an able lawyer. Neither indeed am I altogether convinced, that this habit of multiplying secrets may not be carried on so far as to stop that communication which is necessary, in some degree, among all who have any considerable part in the management of public affairs: because I have observed the inconveniences arising from a want of love between those who were to give directions, to have been of as ill consequence as any that could happen from the discovery of secrets. I suppose, when a building is to be erected, the model may be the contrivance only of one head; and it is sufficient that the under-workmen be ordered to cut stones into certain shapes, and place them in certain positions: but the several masterbuilders must have some general knowledge of the design, without which they can give no orders at all. And, indeed, I do not know a greater mark of an able minister, than that of rightly adapting the several faculties of men; nor is anything more to be lamented, than the impracticableness of doing this in any great degree, under our present circumstances; while so many shut themselves out by adhering to a faction, and while the court is enslaved to the impatience of others, who desire to sell their vote or their interest as dear as they can. But whether this has not been submitted to more than was necessary, whether it has not been dangerous in the example, and pernicious in the practice, I will leave to the inquiry of those who can better determine.

It may be matter of no little admiration to consider, in some lights, the state of affairs among us for four years past. The queen, finding herself and the majority of her kingdom grown weary of the avarice and insolence, the mistaken politics, and destructive principles of her former ministers,[1] calls to the service of the public another set of men, who, by confession of their enemies, had equal abilities at least with their predecessors; whose interest made it necessary for them (although their inclinations had been otherwise) to act upon those maxims which were most agreeable to the constitution in church and state: whose birth and patrimonies gave them weight in the nation; and who (I speak of those who were to have the chief part in affairs) had long lived under the strictest bonds of friendship: with all these advantages, supported by a vast majority of the landed interest, and the inferior clergy almost to a man, we have several times seen the present administration in the greatest distress, and very near the brink of ruin, together with the cause of the church and monarchy committed to their charge; neither does it appear to me at the minute I am now writing, that their power or duration are upon any tolerable foot of security: which I do not so much impute to the address and industry of their enemies, as to some failures among themselves, which I think have been full as visible in their causes as their effects.

[1] *I.e.* the Whigs: this is of course the view of a pronounced Tory.

Nothing has given me greater indignation than to behold a ministry, who came in with the advantages I have represented, acting ever since upon the defensive in the House of Lords, with a majority on their side; and, instead of calling others to account, as it was reasonably expected, misspending their time, and losing many opportunities of doing good, because a struggling faction kept them continually in play. This courage among the adversaries of the court was inspired into them by various incidents, for every one of which I think the ministers, or (if that was the case) the minister[1] alone is to answer.

For, first, that race of politicians, who, in the cant phrase, are called the *whimsicals*,[2] was never so numerous, or at least so active, as it has been since the great change at court; many of those who pretended wholly to be in with the principles upon which her majesty and her new servants proceeded, either absenting themselves with the utmost indifference, in those conjunctures whereon the whole cause depended, or siding directly with the enemy.

I very well remember, when this ministry

[1] Oxford.
[2] The most moderate section of the Tories, who carried their moderation so far as frequently to coalesce with the Whigs.

was not above a year old, there was a little murmuring among such as are called the higher Tories or churchmen, that quicker progress was not made in removing those of the discontented party out of employments. I remember, likewise, the reasonings upon this matter were various, even among many who were allowed to know a good deal of the inside of the court; some supposed the queen was at first prevailed upon to make that great change, with no other view than that of acting for the future upon a moderating scheme, in order to reconcile both parties; and I believe there might possibly have been some grounds for this supposition. Others conceived the employments were left undisposed of, in order to keep alive the hopes of many more impatient candidates than ever could be gratified. This has since been looked on as a very high strain of politics, and to have succeeded accordingly; because it is the opinion of many, that the numerous pretenders to places would never have been kept in order, if all expectation had been cut off. Others were yet more refined; and thought it neither wise nor safe wholly to extinguish all opposition from the other side; because, in the nature of things, it was absolutely necessary that there should be parties in an English parliament;

and a faction already odious to the people might be suffered to continue with less danger than any new one that could arise. To confirm this, it was said, that the majority in the House of Commons was too great on the side of the high-church, and began to form themselves into a body, (by the name of the October Club,)[1] in order to put the ministry under subjection. Lastly, the danger of introducing too great a number of unexperienced men at once into office, was urged as an irrefragable reason for making changes by slow degrees. To discard an able officer from an employment, or part of a commission, where the revenue or trade were concerned, for no other reason but differing in some principles of government, might be of terrible consequence.

However, it is certain that none of these excuses were able to pass among men, who argued only from the principles of general reason. For, first, they looked upon all schemes of comprehension to be as visionary and impossible in the state as in the church. Secondly, while the spirit raised by the trial of Dr Sacheverell[2]

---

[1] An association of the extreme Tories; in 1711 Defoe published a 'Secret History of the October Club.'

[2] Henry Sacheverell, who is described by Mr Lecky as 'an insolent and hot-headed man without learning, literary ability, or real piety,' on 5 Nov. 1709 preached

continued in motion, men were not so keen upon coming in themselves, as to see their enemies out, and deprived of all assistance to do mischief: and it is urged farther, that this general ambition of hunting after places grew chiefly from seeing them so long undisposed of, and from too general an encouragement by promises to all, who were thought capable of doing either good or hurt. Thirdly, the fear of creating another party, in case the present faction were wholly subdued, was, in the opinion of plain men, and in regard to the situation of our affairs, too great a sacrifice of the nation's safety to the genius of politics; considering how much was to be done, and how little time might probably be allowed. Besides, the division of a House of Commons into court and country parties, which was the evil they seemed to apprehend, could never be dangerous to a good ministry, who had the true interest and constitution of their country at heart; as for the apprehension of too great a majority in the House of Commons, it ap-

in St Paul's before the Lord Mayor a sermon in which he inveighed against toleration, insisted on the doctrine of absolute non-resistance, and declared the church was in danger. The House of Commons unwisely determined to impeach Sacheverell. The House of Lords voted him guilty, but the prosecution raised a storm of opposition which finally drove the Whigs from power.

peared to be so vain, that, upon some points of importance, the court was hardly able to procure one. And the October Club, which appeared so formidable at first to some politicians, proved in the sequel to be the chief support of those who suspected them. It was likewise very well known that the greatest part of those men, whom the former ministry left in possession of employments, were loudly charged with insufficiency or corruption, over and above their obnoxious tenets in religion and government; so that it would have been a matter of some difficulty to make a worse choice: beside that the plea for keeping men of factious principles in employment upon the score of their abilities, was thought to be extended a little too far, and construed to take in all employments whatsoever, although many of them required no more abilities than would serve to qualify a gentleman-usher at court:[1] so that this last excuse for the very slow steps made in disarming the adversaries of the crown, was allowed indeed to have more plausibility, but less truth, than any of the former.

I do not here pretend to condemn the counsels

[1] The distinction between permanent and political offices was not at that time established; officials who are now permanent then sometimes went out of office with their party, and *vice versâ*.

or actions of the present ministry: their safety and interest are visibly united with those of the public, they are persons of unquestionable abilities, altogether unsuspected of avarice or corruption, and have the advantage to be farther recommended by the dread and hatred of the opposite faction. However, it is manifest, that the zeal of their friends has been cooling toward them for above two years past: they been have frequently deserted or distressed upon the most pressing occasions, and very near giving up in despair: their characters have often been treated with the utmost barbarity and injustice, in both houses, by scurrilous and enraged orators; while their nearest friends, and even those who must have a share in their disgrace, never offered a word in their vindication.

When I examine with myself what occasions the ministry may have given for this coldness, inconstancy, and discontent among their friends, I at the same time recollect the various conjectures, reasonings, and suspicions, which have run so freely for three years past, concerning the designs of the court: I do not only mean such conjectures as are born in a coffeehouse, or invented by the malice of a party; but also the conclusions (however mistaken) of wise and good men, whose quality and station fitted them to understand the reason of public proceedings, and in whose power it lay to recommend or disgrace an administration to the people. I must therefore take the boldness to assert, that all these discontents, how ruinous soever they may prove in the consequences, have most unnecessarily arisen from the want of a due communication and concert. Every man must have a light sufficient for the length of the way he is appointed to go: there is a degree of confidence due to all stations: and a petty constable will neither act cheerfully nor wisely, without that share of it which properly belongs to him: although the mainspring of a watch be out of sight, there is an intermediate communication between it and the smallest wheel, or else no useful motion could be performed. This reserved mysterious way of acting upon points, where there appeared not the least occasion for it, and towards persons, who, at least in right of their post, expected a more open treatment, was imputed to some hidden design, which every man conjectured to be the very thing he was most afraid of. Those who professed the height of what is called the church principle, suspected that a comprehension was intended wherein the moderate men on both sides might be equally employed. Others went farther, and dreaded such a comprehension, as directly tending to bring the old-exploded principles and persons once more into play. Again, some affected to be uneasy about the succession, and seemed to think there was a view of introducing that person, whatever he is, who pretends to claim the crown by inheritance.[1] Others, especially of late, surmised, on the contrary, that the demands of the House of Hanover were industriously fomented by some in power, without the privity of the ——— or ———. Now, although these accusations were too inconsistent[2] to be all of them true, yet they were maliciously suffered to pass, and thereby took off much of that popularity, of which those at the helm stood in need, to support them under the difficulties of a long perplexing negotiation, a daily addition of public debts, and an exhausted treasury.

But the effects of this mystical manner of

---

[1] That there was such a design is beyond doubt, though Swift was doubtless ignorant of it.

[2] The accusations were inconsistent, but so was the policy of the Government; the extreme Tories suspected Harley of some scheme of comprehension, while the moderate Tories suspected Bolingbroke of Jacobite intrigues.

proceeding did not end here: for the late dissensions between the great men at court (which have been, for some time past, the public entertainment of every coffeehouse) are said to have arisen from the same fountain; while, on one side, very great reserve, and certainly very great resentment on the other, if we may believe general report (for I pretend to know no farther) have inflamed animosities to such a height, as to make all reconcilement impracticable. Supposing this to be true, it may serve for a great lesson of humiliation to mankind, to behold the habits and passions of men, otherwise highly accomplished, triumphing over interest, friendship, honour, and their own personal safety, as well as that of their country, and probably of a most gracious princess, who has entrusted it to them. A ship's crew quarreling in a storm, or while their enemies are within gunshot, is but a faint idea of this fatal infatuation: of which, although it be hard to say enough, some people may think perhaps I have already said too much.

Since this unhappy incident, the desertion of friends, and loss of reputation, have been so great, that I do not see how the ministers could have continued many weeks in their stations, if their opposers of all kinds had agreed about the methods by which they should be ruined: and their preservation hitherto seems to resemble his, who had two poisons given him together of contrary operations.

It may seem very impertinent, in one of my level, to point out to those, who sit at the helm, what course they ought to steer. I know enough of courts to be sensible how mean an opinion great ministers have of most men's understandings: to a degree, that, in any other science, would be called the grossest pedantry. However, unless I offer my sentiments in this point, all I have hitherto said will be to no purpose.

The general wishes and desires of a people are perhaps more obvious to other men than to ministers of state.—There are two points of the highest importance, wherein a very great majority of the kingdom appear perfectly hearty and unanimous. First, that the church of England should be preserved entire in all her rights, powers, and privileges; all doctrines relating to government discouraged, which she condemns; all schisms, sects, and heresies discountenanced, and kept under due subjection, as far as consists with the lenity of our constitution; her open enemies (among whom I include at least dissenters of all denominations) not trusted with the smallest degree of civil or military power; and her secret adversaries, under the names of Whigs, low church, republicans, moderation-men, and the like, receive no marks of favour from the crown, but what they should deserve by a sincere reformation.

Had this point been steadily pursued in all its parts, for three years past, and asserted as the avowed resolution of the court, there must probably have been an end of faction, which has been able, ever since, with so much vigour to disturb and insult the administration. I know very well, that some refiners pretend to argue for the usefulness of parties in such a government as ours; I have said something of this already, and have heard a great many idle wise topics[1] upon the subject. But I shall not argue that matter at present: I suppose if a man think it necessary to play with a serpent, he will choose one of a kind that is least mischievous; otherwise, although it appears to be crushed, it may have life enough to sting him to death. So, I think it is not safe tampering with the present faction, at least in this juncture: first, because their principles and practices have been already very dangerous to the

---

[1] = Arguments.

constitution in church and state: secondly, because they are highly irritated with the loss of their power, full of venom and vengeance, and prepared to execute every thing that rage or malice can suggest: but principally, because they have prevailed, by misrepresentations, and other artifices, to make the successor look upon them as the only persons he can trust: upon which account they cannot be too soon or too much disabled: neither will England ever be safe from the attempts of this wicked confederacy, until their strength and interests shall be so far reduced, that for the future it shall not be in the power of the crown, although in conjunction with any rich and factious body of men, to choose an ill majority in the House of Commons.

One step very necessary to this great work will be, to regulate the army, and chiefly those troops which, in their turns, have the care of her majesty's person; who are most of them fitter to guard a prince under a high court of justice, than seated on the throne. The peculiar hand of Providence has hitherto preserved her majesty, encompassed, whether sleeping or travelling, by her enemies: but since religion teaches us, that Providence ought not to be tempted, it is ill venturing to trust that precious life any longer to those who, by their public behaviour and discourse, discover their impatience to see it at an end; that they may have liberty to be the instruments of glutting at once the revenge of their patrons and their own. It should be well remembered, what a satisfaction these gentlemen (after the example of their betters) were so sanguine to express upon the queen's last illness at Windsor, and what threatenings they used of refusing to obey their general, in case that illness had proved fatal. Nor do I think it a want of charity to suspect, that, in such an evil day, an enraged faction would be highly pleased with the power of the sword, and with great connivance leave it so long unsheathed, until they were got rid of their most formidable adversaries.[1] In the mean time, it must be a very melancholy prospect, that whenever it shall please God to visit us with this calamity, those who are paid to be defenders of the civil power will stand ready for any acts of violence, that a junto, composed of the greatest enemies to the constitution, shall think fit to enjoin them.

[1] The Tories were always suspicious of Marlborough's designs, and hinted that he might imitate Cromwell. "In the latter years of Queen Anne the shadow of Cromwell fell darkly across the path of Marlborough" (Lecky, i. 149).

The other point of great importance is, the security of the Protestant succession in the House of Hanover; not from any partiality to that illustrious house, farther than as it has had the honour to mingle with the blood royal of England, and is the nearest branch of our regal line reformed from popery. This point has one advantage over the former, that both parties profess to desire the same blessing for posterity, but differ about the means of securing it. Whence it has come to pass, that the Protestant succession, in appearance the desire of the whole nation, has proved the greatest topic of slander, jealousy, suspicion, and discontent.

I have been so curious to ask several acquaintances among the opposite party, whether they, or their leaders, did really suspect there had been ever any design in the ministry to weaken the succession in favour of the Pretender, or of any other person whatsoever. Some of them freely answered in the negative: others were of the same opinion, but added, they did not know what might be done in time, and upon further provocations: others again seemed to believe the affirmative, but could never produce any plausible grounds for their belief. I have likewise been assured by a person of some

consequence, that, during a very near and
constant familiarity with the great men at
court for four years past, he never could observe,
even in those hours of conversation
where there is usually least restraint, that one
word ever passed among them to show a dislike
to the present settlement: although they
would sometimes lament, that the false representations
of theirs, and the kingdom's enemies,
had made some impressions in the mind of the
successor. As to my own circle of acquaintance,
I can safely affirm that, excepting those
who are nonjurors by profession, I have not met
with above two persons who appeared to have
any scruples concerning the present limitation
of the crown. I therefore think it may very
impartially be pronounced, that the number
of those, who wish to see the son of the abdicated
prince upon the throne, is altogether
inconsiderable. And farther, I believe it will
be found, that there are none who so much
dread any attempt he shall make for the
recovery of his imagined rights as the Roman
Catholics of England; who love their freedom
and properties too well to desire his entrance
by a French army, and a field of blood; who
must continue upon the same foot, if he changes
his religion, and must expect to be the first

and greatest sufferers, if he should happen to fail.

As to the person of this nominal prince, he lies under all manner of disadvantages; the vulgar imagine him to have been a child imposed upon the nation by the fraudulent zeal of his parents, and their bigoted counsellors; who took special care, against all the rules of common policy, to educate him in their hateful superstition, sucked in with his milk, and confirmed in his manhood, too strongly to be now shaken by Mr Lesley,[1] and a counterfeit conversion will be too gross to pass upon the kingdom, after that we have seen and suffered from the like practice in his father. He is likewise said to be of weak intellectuals, and an unsound constitution; he was treated contemptibly enough by the young princes of France, even during the war; is now wholly neglected by that crown, and driven to live in exile[2] upon a

---

[1] Charles Leslie (1650-1722) an eminent non-juror and pamphleteer. In 1710 his attacks on the Whigs elicited an order for his apprehension and he fled to St Germains. He advised the Pretender not to dissemble his religion but to profess himself open to conviction. In Aug. 1713 he went to Bar-le-Duc where the Pretender gave him a place in his household and promised to listen to his arguments in favour of the Anglican church.

[2] *I.e.* at Bar-le-Duc.

small exhibition; he is utterly unknown in England, which he left in the cradle; his father's friends are most of them dead, the rest antiquated or poor. Six and twenty years have almost past since the Revolution, and the bulk of those who are now most in action either at court, in parliament, or public offices, were then boys at school or the universities, and look upon that great change to have happened during a period of time for which they are not accountable. The logic of the highest Tories is now, that this was the establishment they found, as soon as they arrived at a capacity of judging; that they had no hand in turning out the late king, and therefore had no crime to answer for, if it were any; that the inheritance to the crown is fixed in pursuance of laws made ever since their remembrance, by which all papists are excluded, and they have no other rule to go by; that they will no more dispute King William the Third's title than King William the First's; since they must have recourse to history for both; that they have been instructed in the doctrines of passive obedience, non-resistance, and hereditary right, and find them all necessary for preserving the present establishment in church and state, and for continuing the succession in the house of Hanover, and must in their own opinion renounce all those doctrines by setting up any other title to the crown. This, I say, seems to be the political creed of all the high principled men I have for some time met with of forty years old and under; which, although I do not pretend to justify in every part, yet I am sure it sets the Protestant succession upon a much firmer foundation, than all the indigested schemes of those who profess to act upon what they call Revolution principles.[1]

Neither should it perhaps be soon forgotten, that, during the greatest licentiousness of the press, while the sacred character of the queen was every day insulted in factious papers and ballads, not the least reflecting insinuation ever appeared against the Hanover family, whatever occasion was offered to intemperate pens, by the rashness or indiscretion of one or two ministers from thence.

From all these considerations, I must therefore lay it down as an incontestable truth, that the succession to these kingdoms in the illustrious house of Hanover is as firmly secured as the nature of the thing can pos-

---

[1] It was somewhat on these principles that Bolingbroke subsequently strove to re-construct the Tory party.

sibly admit; by the oaths of all those who are entrusted with any office, by the very principles of those who are termed the high church, by the general inclinations of the people, by the insignificancy of that person who claims it from inheritance, and the little assistance he can expect either from princes abroad, or adherents at home.

However, since the virulent opposers of the queen and her administration have so far prevailed by their emissaries at the court of Hanover, and by their practices upon one or two ignorant unmannerly messengers[1] from thence, as to make the elector desire some farther security, and send over a memorial here to that end; the great question is, how to give reasonable satisfaction to his highness, and (what is infinitely of greater consequence) at the same time consult the honour and safety of the queen, whose quiet possession is of much more consequence to us of the present age, than his reversion. The substance of his memorial, if I retain it right, is, to desire that some one of his family might live in England, with such a maintenance as is usual to those of the royal blood, and that certain titles should be conferred

---

[1] *I.e.* Bothmar and Robethon, Hanoverian envoys, who were in close alliance with the Whigs.

upon the rest, according to ancient custom. The memorial does not specify which of the family should be invited to reside here; and if it had, I believe, however, her majesty would have looked upon it as a circumstance left to her own choice.

But, as all this is most manifestly unnecessary in itself, and only in compliance with the mistaken doubts of a presumptive heir; so the nation would (to speak in the language of Mr Steel) expect, that her majesty should be made perfectly easy from that side for the future; no more to be alarmed with apprehensions of visits, or dreams of writs, where she has not thought fit to give any invitation. The nation would likewise expect, that there should be an end of all private commerce between that court, and the leaders of a party here; and that his electoral highness should declare himself entirely satisfied with all her majesty's proceedings, her treaties of peace and commerce, her alliances abroad, her choice of ministers at home, and particularly in her most gracious condescensions to his request: that he would upon all proper occasions, and in the most public manner, discover his utter dislike of factious persons and principles, but especially of that party, which, under the pretence or shelter of his protection, has so long disquieted the kingdom: and lastly, that he would acknowledge the goodness of the queen, and justice of the nation, in so fully securing the succession to his family.

It is indeed a problem which I could never comprehend, why the court of Hanover, who have all along thought themselves so perfectly secure in the affections, the principles, and the professions of the low church party, should not have endeavoured, according to the usual politics of princes, to gain over those who are represented as their enemies; since these supposed enemies had made so many advances, were in possession of all the power, had framed the very settlement to which that illustrious family owes its claim; had all of them abjured the Pretender; were now employed in the great offices of state, and composed a majority in both houses of parliament. Not to mention, that the queen herself, with the bulk of the landed gentry and commonality throughout the kingdom, were of the number. This, one would think, might be a strength sufficient not only to obstruct, but to bestow a succession: and since the presumed heir could not but be perfectly secure of the other party, whose greatest avowed grievance was the pretended danger of his future rights; it must therefore surely have been worth his while, to have made at least one step toward cultivating a fair correspondence with the power in possession. Neither could those, who are called his friends, have blamed him, or with the least decency enter into any engagements for defeating his title.

But why might not the reasons of this proceeding in the elector be directly contrary to what is commonly imagined? Methinks I could endeavour to believe, that his highness is thoroughly acquainted with both parties; is convinced, that no true member of the church of England can easily be shaken in his principles of loyalty, or forget the obligation of an oath, by any provocation. That these are therefore the people he intends to rely upon, and keeps only fair with the others, from a true notion he has of their doctrines, which prompt them to forget their duty upon every motive of interest or ambition. If this conjecture be right, his highness cannot sure but entertain a very high esteem of such ministers, who continue to act under the dread and appearance of a successor's utmost displeasure, and the threats of an enraged faction, whom he is supposed alone to favour, and to be guided entirely in his judgment of British affairs and persons by their opinions.

But to return from this digression: the presence of that infant prince among us could not, I think, in any sort, be inconsistent with the safety of the queen; he would be in no danger of being corrupted in his principles, or exposed in his person by vicious companions; he could be at the head of no factious clubs and cabals, nor be attended by a hired rabble, which his flatterers might represent as popularity. He would have none of that impatience which the frailty of human nature gives to expecting heirs. There would be no pretence for men to make their court, by affecting German modes and refinements in dress or behaviour: nor would there be any occasion of insinuating to him how much more his levee was frequented than the antechamber of St James's. Add to all this, the advantages of being educated in our religion, laws, language, manners, nature of government, each so very different from those he would leave behind. By which likewise he might be highly useful to his father, if that prince should happen to survive her majesty.

The late King William, who, after his marriage with the Lady Mary of England, could have no probable expectation of the crown, and very little even of being a queen's husband, (the Duke of York having a young wife,) was no stranger to our language or manners, and went often to the chapel of his princess; which I observe the rather, because I could heartily wish the like disposition were in another court, and because it may be disagreeable to a prince to take up new doctrines on a sudden, or speak to his subjects by an interpreter.

An ill-natured or inquisitive man may still, perhaps, desire to press the question farther, by asking what is to be done, in case it should so happen, that this malevolent working party at home has credit enough with the court of Hanover to continue the suspicion, jealousy, and uneasiness there, against the queen and her ministry; to make such demands be still insisted on, as are by no means thought proper to be complied with; and in the mean time to stand at arm's length with her majesty, and in close conjunction with those who oppose her.

I take the answer to be easy: in all contests, the safest way is to put those we dispute with as much in the wrong as we can. When her majesty shall have offered such, or the like concessions, as I have above mentioned, in order to remove those scruples artificially raised in the mind of the expectant heir, and to divide him from that faction by which he is supposed to have been misled; she has done as much as any prince can do, and more than any other would probably do in her case; and will be justified before God and man, whatever be the event. The equitable part of those who now side against the court will probably be more temperate; and if a due dispatch be made in placing the civil and military power in the hands of such as wish well to the constitution, it cannot be any way for the quiet or interest of a successor to gratify so small a faction, as will probably then remain, at the expense of a much more numerous and considerable part of his subjects. Neither do I see how the principles of such a party, either in religion or government, will prove very agreeable, because I think Luther and Calvin[1] seemed to have differed as much as any two among the reformers: and because a German prince will probably be suspicious of those who think they can never depress the prerogative enough.

But supposing, once for all, as far as possible, that the elector should utterly refuse to be upon any terms of confidence with the present ministry, and all others of their principles, as

---

[1] The elector was a Lutheran, and Swift implies that the Low Church party in England were Calvinist.

enemies to him and the succession; nor easy with the queen herself, but upon such conditions as will not be thought consistent with her safety and honour; and continue to place all his hopes and trust in the discontented party; I think it were humbly to be wished, that whenever the succession shall take place, the alterations intended by the new prince should be made by himself, and not by his deputies: because I am of opinion, that the clause empowering the successor to appoint a latent, unlimited number, additional to the seven regents named in the act, went upon a supposition that the secret committee would be of such, whose enmity and contrary principles disposed them to confound the rest. King William, whose title was much more controverted than that of her majesty's successor can ever probably be, did, for several years, leave the administration of the kingdom in the hands of lords justices, during the height of a war, and while the abdicated prince himself was frequently attempting an invasion: whence one might imagine, that the regents appointed by parliament, upon the demise of the crown, would be able to keep the peace during an absence of a few weeks without any colleagues. However, I am pretty confident that the only reason, why a power was given of choosing dormant viceroys, was to take away all pretence of a necessity to invite over any of the family here, during her majesty's life. So that I do not well apprehend what arguments the elector can use to insist upon both.

To conclude: the only way of securing the constitution in church and state, and consequently this very Protestant succession itself, will be by lessening the power of our domestic adversaries as much as can possibly consist with the lenity of our government; and if this be not speedily done, it will be easy to point where the nation is to fix the blame: for we are well assured, that since the account her majesty received of the cabals, the triumphs, the insolent behaviour of the whole faction during her late illness at Windsor, she has been as willing to see them deprived of all power to do mischief, as any of her most zealous and loyal subjects can desire.

VII

THE STATE OF PARTIES AT THE ACCESSION OF GEORGE I

[This pamphlet was written by Henry St John, Viscount Bolingbroke, about 1730. During Queen Anne's reign he had been the leader of those high Tories who would have preferred the succession of the Pretender to that of George I. With that object in view he succeeded in ousting the moderate Harley from office, but Bolingbroke had been Prime Minister for only four days when the Queen died, and no plan for the accession of James III. had been worked out. In fear of attainder Bolingbroke soon after fled to France, but was subsequently allowed to return. He then set to work to reconstruct the Tory party, accepting the Hanoverian succession as a *fait accompli*. His object in this pamphlet is to clear his party and particularly himself from the suspicion of having entertained Jacobite designs, and in order to do this he has no scruples as to the necessity of truth. But it is interesting to see how completely he adopts the views advocated by Swift in 1714 in the preceding pamphlet.][1]

I PERCEIVE by yours that my discourse of the character and conduct of a Patriot King,[2] in that article which relates to *party*, has not

---

[1] See Introduction, p. 19.　　[2] *Ib.*, p. 20.

entirely falsified your expectations. You expected, from some things that I remember to have said to you in conversation, and others that have fallen on that occasion from my pen, a more particular application of those general reasonings to the present time, and to the state of parties, from the late king's[1] accession to the throne. The subject is delicate enough, and yet I shall speak upon it what *truth* exacts from me, with the utmost frankness: for I know all our parties too well to esteem any; and I am too old, and too resigned to my fate, to want or to fear any.

Whatever anecdotes you have been told, for you are too young to have seen the passages of the times I am going to mention, and whatever prepossessions you have had, take these facts for undoubted truths: that there was no design on foot during the last years of Queen Anne's reign to set aside the succession of the house of Hanover, and to place the crown on the head of the pretender to it;[2] nor any

[1] George I.

[2] This statement belies Bolingbroke's pretence of speaking 'what truth exacts'; it is beyond doubt that there was such a design, that Bolingbroke himself was its prime mover, and that only the sudden death of Queen Anne prevented a serious attempt to carry it out. See Macpherson, *Original Papers*, ii. 366-7; *Lockhart Papers*, i. 412, 413; but to admit it at this juncture would have been fatal to Bolingbroke's object.

party formed for this purpose at the time of the death of that princess, whose memory I honour and therefore feel a just indignation at the irreverence with which we have seen it treated. If such a design had been on foot during that time, there were moments when the execution of it would not have been difficult, or dangerous enough, to have stopped men of the most moderate resolution. Neither could a design of that nature have been carried on so long, tho' it was not carried into execution, without leaving some traces, which would have appeared when such strict inquisitions were made; when the papers of so many of the queen's servants were seized, and even her own papers, even those she had sealed up to be burnt after her death were exposed to so much indecent inspection. But laying aside all arguments of the probable kind, I deny the fact absolutely: and I have the better title to expect credit, because it could not be true without my knowledge, or at least suspicion of it; and because even they who believed it, for all who asserted it did not believe it, had no proof to produce, nor have to this hour, but vain surmises; nor any authority to rest upon, but the clamour of party.

That there were particular men, who corresponded indirectly and directly too with the pretender, and with others for his service; that these men professed themselves to be zealous in it, and made large promises, and raised some faint hopes, I cannot doubt; tho' this was unknown to me at that time, or at least I knew it not with the same certainty and in the same detail that I have known it since. But if this were done by some who were in the queen's service, it was done too by some who were out of it,[1] and I think with little sincerity by either.

It may well seem strange to one who carries in his breast a heart like yours, that men of any rank, and especially of the highest, should hold a conduct so false, so dangerous, always of uncertain event, and often, as it was in the case here mentioned, upon remote contingencies, and such as they themselves think the least probable. Even I think it strange, who have been much longer mingled in a corrupt world, and who have seen many more examples of the folly, of the cunning, and the perfidy of mankind. A great regard to wealth, and a total contempt of virtue, are sentiments

---

[1] *E.g.* Marlborough, who was in correspondence with the Courts of Hanover and St Germains at the same time.

very nearly allied: and they must possess the whole souls of men whom they can determine to such infamous duplicity, to such double treachery. In fact they do so. *One* is so afraid of losing his fortune, that he lays in claims to secure it, perhaps to augment it, on all sides, and to prevent even imaginary dangers. *Another* values so little the inward testimony of a good conscience, or the future reproaches of those he has deceived, that he scruples not to take engagements for a time to come that he has no design to keep; if they may serve as expedients to facilitate, in any small degree, the success of an immediate project. All this was done at the time, on the occasion, and by the persons I intend. But the scheme of defeating the Protestant succession was so far from being laid by the queen and her ministers,[1] and such a resolution was so far from being taken, that the very men I speak of, when they were pressed by the other side, that is from Versailles and St Germains, to be more particular, and to come into a closer concert, declined both, and gave the most evasive answers.

---

[1] Queen Anne of course had nothing to do with the Jacobite designs, and the statement about her ministers is true if applied to Harley.

A little before, or about the time of the queen's death, some other persons, who figured afterwards in the rebellion,[1] entered in good earnest into those engagements, as I believe; for I do not know exactly the date of them. But whenever they took them, they took them as *single* men. They could answer for no *party* to back them. They might flatter themselves with hopes and dreams like Pompey, if little men and little things may be compared with great, of legions ready to rise at the stamp of their feet.[2] But they had no assurance, no nor grounds to expect any troops, except those of the highlands, whose disposition in general was known to every man, but whose insurrection without the concurrence of other insurrections, and other troops, was deemed, even by those that made them take arms afterwards, not a strength but a weakness, ruin to the poor people, and ruin to the cause. In a word these men were so truly single in their engagements, and their measures were so unripe for action when the resolution of acting immediately was taken by them, that

---

[1] *E.g.* The Earl of Mar.

[2] In the year 49 B.C., just before the outbreak of the war between Cæsar and Pompey, the latter asserted that he had only to stamp his foot to cover the ground with armed men. See Mommsen, iv. 371.

I am persuaded they durst not communicate their design to any one man of consequence that served at that time with them. What persuades me of it is this: one man, whom they thought likely to incline to them on several accounts, they attempted indirectly and at a great distance: they came no nearer to the point with him, neither then, that is just before the queen's death, nor afterwards. They had indeed no encouragement to do it; for upon this hint and another circumstance which fell in, both he and others took several occasions to declare that tho' they would serve the queen faithfully and exclusively of all other regards or engagements to her last breath, yet after her decease they would acknowledge the prince on whom the succession devolved by law, and to which they had sworn, and no other. This declaration would have been that of the far greatest number of the same party, and would have been stuck to by them, if the passions and private interests of *another party* had not prevailed over the true interest of a new family that was going to mount the throne. You may ask me now, and the question will not be at all improper, how it came to pass, if the queen and her ministers had no design to defeat this succession, that so much suspicion of it prevailed, that so great an alarm was taken, and so great a clamour raised? I might answer you very shortly and very truly, by the strange conduct of a first minister,[1] by the contests about the negotiations of the peace, and by the arts of a party.

The minds of some ministers are like the *sanctum sanctorum* of a temple I have read of somewhere: before it a great curtain was solemnly drawn; within it nothing was to be seen but a confused group of miss-shapen, and imperfect forms, heads without bodies, bodies without heads and the like. To develop the most complicated cases, and to decide in the most doubtful, has been the talent of great ministers: it is that of others to perplex the most simple, and to be puzzled by the plainest. No man was more desirous of power than the minister here intended: and he had a competent share of cunning to wriggle himself into it: but then his part was over, and no man was more at a loss how to employ it. The ends he proposed to himself, he saw for the most part darkly and indistinctly: and if he saw them a little better, he still made use of means disproportionate to them. That

---

[1] Harley: the following paragraph is a severe, but not altogether inaccurate, characterisation of that minister.

private correspondence with the queen, which produced the change of ministry in 1710, was begun with him whilst he was secretary of state, and was continued thro' him during the two years that intervened between his leaving the court, and his return to it. This gave him the sole confidence of the queen, put him more absolutely at the head of the party that came into power, and invested him with all the authority that a first minister could have in those days, and before any man could presume to rival in that rank, and in this kingdom, the rank of the ancient mayors of the palace in France.[1] The tories, with whom and by whom he had risen, expected much from him. Their expectations were ill-answered: and I think that such management as he employed would not have hindered them long from breaking from him, if new things had not fallen in, to engage their whole attention, and to divert their passions.

The foolish prosecution of Sacheverel[2] had carried party-rage to the height, and the late change of the ministry had confirmed it

---

[1] Bolingbroke insinuates that Walpole, the prime minister at the date at which he was writing, was like a mayor of the palace, and the king by implication a *roi fainéant*.

[2] See pp. 145, 146.

there. These circumstances, and many others relative to them, which I omit, would have made it impossible, if there had been honesty and wisdom enough to desire it, to bring about a coalition of the bulk of the tories and whigs at the latter end of this reign: as it had been brought about a few years before under the administration of my lord Marlborough and my lord Godolphin, who broke it soon and before it had time to cement, by making such an use of it, as I am unable to account for even at this hour. The two parties were in truth become factious, in the strict sense of the word. I was of one, and I own the guilt; which no man of the other would have a good grace to deny. In this respect they were alike; but here was the difference: one was well united, well conducted, and determined to their future, as well as their present objects. Not one of these advantages attended the other. The minister had evidently no bottom to rest his administration upon, but that of the party, at the head of which he came into power: if he had gained their confidence, instead of creating even wantonly, if I may say so, a distrust of himself in them, it is certain he might have determined them to every national interest during the queen's time, and after her death. But this was above his conception as well as his talents. He meant to keep power as long as he could, by the little arts by which he had got into it; he thought that he should be able to compound for himself in all events, and cared little what became of his party, his mistress, or the nation. That this was the whole of his scheme appeared sufficiently in the course of his administration; was then seen by some, and has been since acknowledged by all people. For this purpose he coaxed and persecuted whigs, he flattered and disappointed tories; and supported by a thousand little tricks his tottering administration. To the tory party he held out the peace, as an œra when all they expected should be done for them, and when they should be placed in such fulness of power and such strength of party, *that it would be more the interest of the successor to be well with them, than theirs to be well with him.* Such expressions were often used, and others of like import: and I believe these oracular speeches were interpreted, as oracles used to be, according as every man's inclinations led him.

The contests that soon followed, by the

violent opposition to the negotiations of peace, did the good hinted at above to the minister, and enabled him to amuse and banter his party a little longer. But they did great, and in some respects irreparable, mischief to Great Britain, and to all Europe. One part of the mischief they did at home is proper to be mentioned here. They dipped the house of Hanover in our party-quarrels unseasonably, I presume to think, and unpopularly: for tho' the contest was maintained by two parties that pretended equally to have the national interest at heart, yet the national interest was so plainly on one side of the question, and the other side was so plainly partial, at the expense of this interest, to the emperor, the princes of the empire, and the Dutch in particular; that a successor to the crown, who was himself a prince of Germany, should have preserved in good policy, for this very reason, the appearance at least of some neutrality. The means employed openly to break the queen's measures were indecent and unjustifiable: those employed secretly, and meditated to be employed, were worse. The ministers of Hanover, whose conduct I may censure the more freely because the late king did not approve it all, took so remarkable a share in the first, that they might be, and they were, suspected of having some in the others. This had a very bad effect, which was improved by men in the two extremes. The whigs desired nothing more than to have it thought that the successor was theirs, if I may repeat an insolent expression which was used at that time: the notion did them honour, and tho' it could give no colour, it gave some strength to their opposition. The Jacobites insinuated industriously the same thing; and represented that the establishment of the house of Hanover would be the establishment of the whig party, and that the interests of Great Britain would be constantly sacrificed to foreign interests, and her wealth drained to support them under that family. I leave you to judge what ingression such exaggerations must find, on such occasion, and in such a ferment. I do not think they determined men to Jacobitism. I know they did not; but I know that they dis-inclined men from the succession, and made many who resolved to submit to it, submit to it rather as a necessary evil, than as an eligible good.

This was, to the best of my observation, and knowledge, the state of one party. An absurd one it was, and the consequences of it were foreseen, foretold, and pressed upon the minister at the time, but always without effect, and sometimes without any answers. He had some private intrigue for himself at Hanover: so he had at Bar.[1] He was the bubble of one in the end: the pretender was so of the other. But his whole management in the mean time was contrived to keep up a kind of general indetermination in the party about the succession; which made a man of great temper once say to him with passion, that 'he believed no other minister at the head of a powerful party would not be better at Hanover, if he did not mean to be worse there.'

The state of the other party was this. The whigs had appeared zealous for the Protestant succession from the time when king William proposed it, after the death of the duke of Gloucester.[2] The tories voted for it then, and the acts that were judged necessary to secure it, some of them at least, were promoted by them. Yet they were not thought, nor did they affect as the others did, to be thought extremely fond of it. King William did not come into this

---

[1] One of the provisions of the Treaty of Utrecht was that the Pretender should be expelled from France, and he then established his court at Bar-le-Duc in Lorraine.

[2] The husband of Princess (afterwards Queen) Anne.

measure, till he found, upon trial, that there was no other safe and practicable: and the tories had an air of coming into it for no other reason. Besides which, it is certain that there was at that time a much greater leaven of Jacobitism in the tory-lump, than at the time spoken of here.

Now thus far the whigs acted like a national party, who thought that their religion and liberty could be secured by no other expedient, and therefore adhered to this settlement of the crown with distinguished zeal. But this national party degenerated soon into faction; that is, the national interest became soon a secondary and subservient motive, and the cause of the succession was supported more for the sake of the party or faction, than for the sake of the nation; and with views that went more directly to the establishment of their own administration, than to a solid settlement of the present royal family. This appeared, evidently enough, to those whom noise and show could not impose on, in the latter end of the queen's reign, and plain beyond dispute to all mankind, after her decease. The art of the whigs was to blend, as undistinguishably as they could, all their party-interests with those of the succession; and they made the same factious use of the supposed danger of it, as the Tories had endeavoured to make some time before of the supposed danger of the church. As no man is reputed a friend to Christianity beyond the Alps and the Pyrenees, who does not acknowledge the papal supremacy, so here no man was to be reputed a friend to the Protestant succession who was not ready to acknowledge their supremacy. The interest of the present royal family was to succeed without opposition and risk, and to come to the throne in a calm. It was the interest of a faction that they should come to it in a storm. Accordingly the whigs were very near putting in execution some of the wildest projects of insurrections and rebellion, under pretence of securing what there was not sufficient disposition, nor any preparation at all made to obstruct. Happily for the public these designs proved abortive. They were too well known to have succeeded, but they might have had, and they would have had, most fatal consequences. The storm, that was not raised to disturb and endanger the late king's accession, was only deferred. To a party, who meant nothing less than engrossing the whole power of the government and the whole wealth of the nation under the successor, a storm, in which every other man should be driven from him, was too necessary, not to be conjured up at any rate; and it was so immediately after the late king's accession. He came to the throne easily, and quietly, and took possession of the kingdom with as little trouble, as he could have expected if he had been not only the queen's successor, but her son. The whole nation submitted cheerfully to his government, and the queen's servants discharged the duty of their offices, whilst he continued them in their offices, in such a manner as to merit his approbation. This was signified to some of them, to the secretaries in particular, in the strongest terms, and according to his majesty's express order, before the whole council of state. He might I think, I thought then that he ought, and every man except the earl of O——d,[1] who believed or had a mind to make others believe that his influence would be great in the new reign, expected that he would have given his principal confidence and the principal power of the administration to the whigs: but it was scarce possible to expect, that he would immediately let loose the whole fury of party, suffer the queen's servants, who had surely

[1] Robert Harley, Earl of Oxford.

been guilty of no crime against him or the state, to be so bitterly persecuted; and proscribe in effect every man in the country who did not bear the name of whig. Princes have often forgot, on their accession to a throne, even personal injuries received in party quarrels: and the saying of Lewis XII. of France, in answer to those who would have persuaded him to show severity to La Tremouille, is very deservedly famous. 'God forbid,' said he, 'that Lewis XII. should revenge the quarrels of the duke of Orleans.'[1] Other princes, who have fought their way to the throne, have not only exercised clemency, but shown favour to those who had stood in arms against them: and here again I might quote the example of another king of France, that of Henry IV. But to take an example in our own country, look back to the restoration, consider all that passed from the year 1641 to the year 1660, and then compare the measures that King Charles the second was advised to pursue for the establishment of his government in the circumstances of that time, with those which the late king was advised, and prevailed on, against his opinion, inclination, and first resolution, to

---

[1] He was Duke of Orleans before he came to the throne.

pursue, in the circumstances I have just mentioned. I leave the conclusion to the candour and good sense of every impartial reader.

To these measures of unexpected violence alone must it be ascribed, that the pretender had any party for him of strength sufficient to appear and act. These measures alone produced the troubles that followed, and dyed the royal ermines of a prince, in no way sanguinary, in blood. I am far from excusing one party, for suffering another to drive them into rebellion. I wish I could forget it myself. But there are two observations on that event, which I cannot refuse myself to make. One is, that the very manner in which this rebellion was begun shews abundantly that it was a start of passion, a sudden phrenzy of men transported by their resentment, and nothing less[1] than the execution of a design long premeditated and prepared. The other is, that few examples are to be found in history, perhaps none, of what happened on this occasion, when the same men, in the same

---

[1] Ordinary use makes 'nothing less' equivalent to 'nothing but'; this interpretation would make the passage meaningless, and the real sense is that nothing was less the execution of a design than the rebellion.

country, and in the compass of the same year, were ready to rise in arms against one prince without any national cause; and then provoked, by the violence of their councils, the opposite faction to rise in actual rebellion against the successor.

These are some of the effects of maintaining *divisions* in a nation, and of *governing* by *faction*. I might descend into a detail of many fatal consequences that have followed, from the first false step which was taken, when the present settlement was so avowedly made on the *narrow bottom* of *party*. But I consider that this discourse is growing into length; that I have had and shall have occasion to mention some of these consequences elsewhere; and that your own reflections on what has been said, will more than supply what I omit to say in this place. Let me therefore conclude by repeating, that *division* has caused all the mischief we lament, that *union* can alone retrieve it, and that a great advance towards this union was the coalition of parties, so happily begun, so successfully carried on, and of late so unaccountably neglected, to say no worse. But let me add, that this union can never be complete, till it become an union of the *head* with the *members,* as well as of the members with one another: and that such an union can never be expected till *patriotism* fills the *throne,* and *faction* be banished from the *administration.*

VIII

THE DRAPIER'S LETTERS

[The fourth of these letters reprinted here is the most famous of Swift's Irish writings. On 12 July 1722 one ironmonger named William Wood was granted a patent to coin £400,000 worth of copper coins to replace those then in use in Ireland. It at once roused a great outcry in Ireland ; there it was believed that the measure would drive all silver and gold coin out of the kingdom and that Ireland would be ruined. It was beyond doubt that the amount was far in excess of what was required. Then, as has happened since, a financial question united all classes in opposition to the English government. Swift threw himself into the fray and assuming the guise of a Dublin tradesman wrote his 'Drapier's Letters.' 'In his famous fourth letter,' writes Mr Lecky, 'he re-asserted with commanding power the principles of Molyneux ; claimed for the Irish Legislature the right of self-government ; drew with a firm and unfaltering hand the line between the prerogative of the Sovereign and the liberty of the people ; laid bare the scandalous abuses of the Irish Government ; and, urging that "'government without the consent of the governed is the very definition of slavery,'" struck a chord which for the first time vibrated through every class in Ireland.][1]

[1] *History of Ireland*, ed. 1892, i. 454.

LETTER IV

TO
THE WHOLE PEOPLE OF IRELAND

October 23, 1724.

MY DEAR COUNTRYMEN,—Having already written three letters upon so disagreeable a subject as Mr Wood and his halfpence, I conceived my task was at an end; but I find that cordials must be frequently applied to weak constitutions, political as well as natural. A people long used to hardships lose by degrees the very notions of liberty. They look upon themselves as creatures at mercy, and that all impositions, laid on them by a stronger hand, are, in the phrase of the Report,[1] legal and obligatory. Hence proceed that poverty and lowness of spirit, to which a kingdom may be subject, as well as a particular person. And when Esau came fainting from the field at the point to die, it is no wonder that he sold his birthright for a mess of pottage.

I thought I had sufficiently shewn, to all who could want instruction, by what methods

---

[1] *I.e.* the report of the Committee of the Privy Council, dated 24 July 1724. The Committee had been appointed to consider the complaints against Wood's patent.

they might safely proceed, whenever this coin should be offered to them; and, I believe, there has not been, for many ages, an example of any kingdom so firmly united in a point of great importance, as this of ours is at present against that detestable fraud. But, however, it so happens, that some weak people begin to be alarmed anew by rumours industriously spread. Wood prescribes to the newsmongers in London what they are to write. In one of their papers, published here by some obscure printer, and certainly with a bad design, we are told, 'That the Papists in Ireland have entered into an association against his coin,' although it be notoriously known, that they never once offered to stir in the matter; so that the two Houses of Parliament, the Privy-council, the great number of corporations, the lord mayor and aldermen of Dublin, the grand juries, and principal gentlemen of several counties, are stigmatized in a lump under the name of 'Papists.'

This impostor and his crew do likewise give out, that, by refusing to receive his dross for sterling, we 'dispute the king's prerogative, are grown ripe for rebellion, and ready to shake off the dependency of Ireland upon the crown of England.' To countenance which reports, he has published a paragraph in another newspaper, to let us know, that 'the Lord-lieutenant [1] is ordered to come over immediately to settle his halfpence.'

I entreat you, my dear countrymen, not to be under the least concern upon these and the like rumours, which are no more than the last howls of a dog dissected alive, as I hope he has sufficiently been. These calumnies are the only reserve that is left him. For surely our continued and (almost) unexampled loyalty, will never be called in question, for not suffering ourselves to be robbed of all that we have by one obscure ironmonger.

As to disputing the King's prerogative, give me leave to explain, to those who are ignorant, what the meaning of that word *prerogative* is.

The Kings of these realms enjoy several powers, wherein the laws have not interposed. So, they can make war and peace without the consent of Parliament — and this is a very great prerogative: but if the Parliament does not approve of the war, the King must bear the charge of it out of his own purse—and

---

[1] Carteret; the former Lord-lieutenant Grafton had been recalled because he was thought too weak to deal with the crisis. Carteret, however, fared little better.

this is a great check on the crown. So, the
King has a prerogative to coin money without
consent of Parliament; but he cannot compel
the subject to take that money, except it be
sterling gold or silver, because herein he is
limited by law. Some princes have, indeed,
extended their prerogative farther than the
law allowed them; wherein, however, the
lawyers of succeeding ages, as fond as they
are of precedents, have never dared to justify
them. But, to say the truth, it is only of
late times that prerogative has been fixed and
ascertained; for, whoever reads the history of
England will find, that some former Kings,
and those none of the worst, have, upon
several occasions, ventured to control the
laws, with very little ceremony or scruple,
even later than the days of Queen Elizabeth.
In her reign, that pernicious counsel of sending
base money hither, very narrowly failed of
losing the kingdom[1]—being complained of by
the lord-deputy, the council, and the whole
body of the English here; so that, soon after
her death, it was recalled by her successor, and
lawful money paid in exchange.

Having thus given you some notion of what
is meant by 'the King's prerogative,' as far as

[1] *I.e.* during Tyrone's rebellion, 1600-01.

a tradesman can be thought capable of explaining it, I will only add the opinion of the great Lord Bacon: 'That, as God governs the world by the settled laws of nature, which he has made, and never transcends those laws but upon high important occasions, so, among earthly princes, those are the wisest and the best, who govern by the known laws of the country, and seldomest make use of their prerogative.' [1]

Now here you may see, that the vile accusation of Wood and his accomplices, charging us with disputing the King's prerogative by refusing his brass, can have no place—because compelling the subject to take any coin which is not sterling, is no part of the King's prerogative, and, I am very confident, if it were so, we should be the last of his people to dispute it; as well from that inviolable loyalty we have always paid to his Majesty, as from the treatment we might, in such a case, justly expect from some, who seem to think we have neither common sense, nor common senses. But, God be thanked, the best of them are only our fellow-subjects, and not our masters. One great merit I am sure we have, which

---

[1] A paraphrase of some of Bacon's ideas, not an exact quotation from him.

those of English birth can have no pretence to—that our ancestors reduced this kingdom to the obedience of England; for which we have been rewarded with a worse climate,—the privilege of being governed by laws to which we do not consent,—a ruined trade,—a House of Peers without jurisdiction,—almost an incapacity for all employments,—and the dread of Wood's halfpence.

But we are so far from disputing the King's prerogative in coining, that we own he has power to give a patent to any man for setting his royal image and superscription upon whatever materials he pleases, and liberty to the patentee to offer them in any country from England to Japan; only attended with one small limitation—that nobody alive is obliged to take them.

Upon these considerations, I was ever against all recourse to England for a remedy against the present impending evil; especially when I observed, that the addresses of both Houses, after long expectance, produced nothing but a REPORT, altogether in favour of Wood; upon which I made some observations in a former letter, and might at least have made as many more, for it is a paper of as singular a nature as I ever beheld.

But I mistake; for, before this Report was made, his Majesty's most gracious answer to the House of Lords was sent over, and printed; wherein are these words, granting the patent for coining halfpence and farthings, AGREEABLE TO THE PRACTICE OF HIS ROYAL PREDECESSORS, &c. That King Charles II. and King James II. (AND THEY ONLY,) did grant patents for this purpose, is indisputable, and I have shewn it at large. Their patents were passed under the great seal of Ireland, by references to Ireland; the copper to be coined in Ireland; the patentee was bound, on demand, to receive his coin back in Ireland, and pay silver and gold in return. Wood's patent was made under the great seal of England; the brass coined in England; not the least reference made to Ireland; the sum immense, and the patentee under no obligation to receive it again, and give good money for it. This I only mention, because, in my private thoughts, I have sometimes made a query, whether the penner of those words in his Majesty's most gracious answer, 'agreeable to the practice of his royal predecessors,' had maturely considered the several circumstances, which, in my poor opinion, seem to make a difference.

Let me now say something concerning the

other great cause of some people's fear, as Wood has taught the London newswriter to express it, that his Excellency the Lord-lieutenant is coming over to settle Wood's halfpence.

We know very well, that the Lords-lieutenants, for several years past, have not thought this kingdom worthy the honour of their residence longer than was absolutely necessary for the King's business, which, consequently, wanted no speed in the dispatch. And therefore it naturally fell into most men's thoughts, that a new governor, coming at an unusual time, must portend some unusual business to be done; especially if the common report be true, that the Parliament, prorogued to I know not when, is by a new summons, revoking that prorogation, to assemble soon after the arrival; for which extraordinary proceeding, the lawyers on the other side the water have, by great good fortune, found two precedents.

All this being granted, it can never enter into my head, that so little a creature as Wood would find credit enough with the King and his ministers, to have the Lord-lieutenant of Ireland sent hither in a hurry upon his errand.

For, let us take the whole matter nakedly as it lies before us, without the refinements of some people with which we have nothing to do. Here is a patent granted under the great seal of England, upon false suggestions, to one William Wood, for coining copper halfpence for Ireland. The Parliament here, upon apprehensions of the worst consequences from the said patent, address the King to have it recalled. This is refused; and a committee of the Privy-council report to his Majesty, that Wood has performed the conditions of his patent. He then is left to do the best he can with his halfpence, no man being obliged to receive them; the people here, being likewise left to themselves, unite as one man, resolving they will have nothing to do with his ware.

By this plain account of the fact it is manifest, that the King and his ministry are wholly out of the case, and the matter is left to be disputed between him and us. Will any man, therefore, attempt to persuade me, that a Lord-lieutenant is to be dispatched over in great haste before the ordinary time, and a Parliament summoned by anticipating a prorogation, merely to put a hundred thousand pounds into the pocket of a sharper, by the ruin of a most loyal kingdom?

But, supposing all this to be true, by what arguments could a Lord-lieutenant prevail on the same Parliament which addressed with so much zeal and earnestness against this evil, to pass it into a law? I am sure their opinion of Wood and his project is not mended since their last prorogation; and, supposing those methods should be used, which detractors tell us have been sometimes put in practice for gaining votes, it is well known, that, in this kingdom, there are few employments to be given; and, if there were more, it is as well known to whose share they must fall.

But, because great numbers of you are altogether ignorant of the affairs of your country, I will tell you some reasons why there are so few employments to be disposed of in this kingdom.

All considerable offices for life are here possessed by those to whom the reversions were granted; and these have been generally followers of the chief governors, or persons who had interest in the Court of England. So, the Lord Berkeley of Stratton holds that great office of master of the rolls; the Lord Palmerstown is first remembrancer, worth near £2000 per annum. One Dodington, secretary to the Earl of Pembroke, begged the reversion of clerk of the pells, worth £2500 a year, which he now enjoys by the death of the Lord Newtown. Mr Southwell is secretary of state, and the Earl of Burlington lord high treasurer of Ireland by inheritance. These are only a few among many others which I have been told of, but cannot remember. Nay, the reversion of several employments, during pleasure, is granted the same way. This, among others, is a circumstance, whereby the kingdom of Ireland is distinguished from all other nations upon earth; and makes it so difficult an affair to get into a civil employ, that Mr Addison was forced to purchase an old obscure place, called keeper of the records in Bermingham's Tower, of £10 a-year, and to get a salary of £400 annexed to it, though all the records there are not worth half-a-crown, either for curiosity or use. And we lately saw a favourite secretary descend to be master of the revels, which, by his credit and extortion, he has made pretty considerable. I say nothing of the under-treasurership, worth about £9000 a-year, nor of the commissioners of the revenue, four of whom generally live in England, for I think none of these are granted in reversion. But the jest is, that I have known, upon occasion, some of these absent officers as keen against the interest of Ireland, as if they had never been indebted to her for a single groat.

I confess, I have been sometimes tempted to

wish, that this project of Wood's might succeed; because I reflected with some pleasure, what a jolly crew it would bring over among us of lords and squires, and pensioners of both sexes, and officers civil and military, where we should live together as merry and sociable as beggars; only with this one abatement, that we should neither have meat to feed, nor manufactures to clothe us, unless we could be content to prance about in coats of mail, or eat brass as ostriches do iron.

I return from this digression to that which gave me the occasion of making it. And I believe you are now convinced, that if the Parliament of Ireland were as temptable as any other assembly within a mile of Christendom, (which God forbid!) yet the managers must of necessity fail for want of tools to work with. But I will yet go one step farther, by supposing that a hundred new employments were erected on purpose to gratify compliers; yet still an insuperable difficulty would remain. For it happens, I know not how, that money is neither Whig nor Tory—neither of town nor country party; and it is not improbable, that a gentleman would rather choose to live upon his own estate, which brings him gold and silver, than with the addition of an employment, when his rents and salary must both be paid in Wood's brass, at above eighty per cent. discount.

For these, and many other reasons, I am confident you need not be under the least apprehension from the sudden expectation of the Lord-lieutenant, while we continue in our present hearty disposition, to alter which no suitable temptation can possibly be offered. And if, as I have often asserted from the best authority, the law has not left a power in the crown to force any money, except sterling, upon the subject, much less can the crown devolve such a power upon another.

This I speak with the utmost respect to the person and dignity of his excellency the Lord Carteret, whose character was lately given me by a gentleman that has known him from his first appearance in the world. That gentleman describes him as a young nobleman of great accomplishments, excellent learning, regular in his life, and of much spirit and vivacity. He has since, as I have heard, been employed abroad; was principal secretary of state; and is now, about the thirty-seventh year of his age, appointed Lord-lieutenant of Ireland. From such a governor, this kingdom may reasonably hope for as much prosperity, as, under so many discouragements, it can be capable of receiving.

It is true, indeed, that, within the memory of man, there have been governors of so much dexterity, as to carry points of terrible consequence to this kingdom, by their power with those who are in office; and by their arts in managing or deluding others with oaths, affability, and even with dinners. If Wood's brass had in those times been upon the anvil, it is obvious enough to conceive what methods would have been taken. Depending persons would have been told in plain terms, 'that it was a service expected from them, under the pain of the public business being put into more complying hands.' Others would be allured by promises. To the country gentlemen, beside good words, burgundy, and closeting, it might perhaps have been hinted, 'how kindly it would be taken to comply with a royal patent, although it were not compulsory; that if any inconveniences ensued, it might be made up with other graces or favours hereafter; that gentlemen ought to consider whether it were prudent or safe to disgust England. They would be desired to think of some good bills for encouraging of trade, and setting the poor to work; some farther acts against Popery, and for uniting Protestants.' There would be solemn engagements, 'that we should never be troubled with above forty thousand pounds in his coin, and all of the best and weightiest sort, for which we should only give our manufactures in exchange, and keep our gold and silver at home.' Perhaps a seasonable report of some invasion would have been spread in the most proper juncture; which is a great smoother of rubs in public proceedings; and we should have been told, 'that this was no time to create differences, when the kingdom was in danger.'

These, I say, and the like methods, would, in corrupt times, have been taken to let in this deluge of brass among us; and I am confident, even then, would not have succeeded; much less under the administration of so excellent a person as the Lord Carteret; and in a country where the people of all ranks, parties, and denominations, are convinced to a man, that the utter undoing of themselves and their posterity for ever, will be dated from the admission of that execrable coin; that if it once enters, it can be no more confined to a small or moderate quantity, than a plague can be confined to a few families; and that no equivalent can be given by any earthly power, any more than a dead carcass can be recovered to life by a cordial.

There is one comfortable circumstance in this universal opposition to Mr Wood, that the people sent over hither from England, to fill up our vacancies, ecclesiastical, civil, and military, are all on our side. Money, the great divider of the world, has, by a strange revolution, been the great uniter of a most divided people.[1] Who would leave a hundred pounds a-year in England (a country of freedom) to be paid a thousand in Ireland out of Wood's exchequer? The gentleman [2] they have lately made primate, would never quit his seat in an English House of Lords, and his preferments at Oxford and Bristol, worth twelve hundred pounds a-year, for four times the denomination here, but not half the value; therefore I expect to hear he will be as good an Irishman, at least upon this one article, as any of his brethren, or even of us, who have had the misfortune to be born in this island.[3] For, those who in the common phrase do not come hither to learn

---

[1] The aptness of this remark needs no emphasising to-day.

[2] Dr Hugh Boulter (1672-1742).

[3] This anticipation proved correct. See Lecky's *Hist. Ireland*, i. 455.

the language, would never change a better country for a worse, to receive brass instead of gold.

Another slander spread by Wood and his emissaries, is, 'that by opposing him, we discover an inclination to throw off our dependence upon the crown of England.' Pray observe how important a person is this same William Wood, and how the public weal of two kingdoms is involved in his private interest. First, all those who refuse to take his coin are Papists; for he tells us, 'that none but Papists are associated against him.' Secondly, 'they dispute the King's prerogative.' Thirdly, 'they are ripe for rebellion.' And, fourthly, 'they are going to shake off their dependence upon the crown of England;' that is to say, they are going to choose another king; for there can be no other meaning in this expression, however some may pretend to strain it.

And this gives me an opportunity of explaining to those who are ignorant, another point, which has often swelled in my breast. Those who come over hither to us from England, and some weak people among ourselves, whenever in discourse we make mention of liberty and property, shake their heads, and tell us, that 'Ireland is a depending kingdom;'

as if they would seem by this phrase to intend, that the people of Ireland are in some state of slavery or dependence different from those of England: whereas a depending kingdom is a modern term of art, unknown as I have heard to all ancient civilians, and writers upon government; and Ireland is, on the contrary, called in some statutes 'an imperial crown,' as held only from God; which is as high a style as any kingdom is capable of receiving. Therefore, by this expression, 'a depending kingdom,' there is no more to be understood, than that, by a statute made here in the thirty-third year of Henry VIII.,[1] the King, and his successors, are to be kings imperial of this realm, as united and knit to the imperial crown of England. I have looked over all the English and Irish statutes, without finding any law that makes Ireland depend upon England, any more than England does upon Ireland. We have indeed obliged ourselves to have the same king with them; and consequently they are obliged to have the same king with us. For the law was made by our own Parliament; and our ancestors then were not such fools (whatever they were in the preceding reign) to bring themselves under I

---

[1] Really in 1543, the 35th year of Henry VIII.

know not what dependence, which is now talked of, without any ground of law, reason, or common sense.[1]

Let whoever thinks otherwise I, M. B., drapier, desire to be excepted; for I declare, next under God, I depend only on the King my sovereign, and on the laws of my own country. And I am so far from depending upon the people of England, that if they should ever rebel against my sovereign (which God forbid!) I would be ready, at the first command from his Majesty, to take arms against them, as some of my countrymen did against theirs at Preston. And if such a rebellion should prove so successful as to fix the Pretender on the throne of England, I would venture to transgress that statute so far, as to lose every drop of my blood to hinder him from being King of Ireland.

It is true, indeed, that within the memory

---

[1] This is scarcely an accurate account of the position of Ireland. Poynings' Act passed in 1494 really placed the Irish Parliament in a subordinate position by extending to Ireland the scope of all acts passed in the English Parliament and making the consent of the English Privy Council necessary for the validity of Irish Statutes. In 1719 an act was also passed enabling the English Parliament to legislate for Ireland. These measures were repealed in 1782, when Ireland was given full legislative independence.

of man, the Parliaments of England have sometimes assumed the power of binding this kingdom by laws enacted there; wherein they were at first openly opposed (as far as truth, reason, and justice, are capable of opposing) by the famous Mr Molineux,[1] an English gentleman born here, as well as by several of the greatest patriots and best Whigs in England; but the love and torrent of power prevailed. Indeed the arguments on both sides were invincible. For, in reason, all government without the consent of the governed, is the very definition of slavery; but, in fact, eleven men well armed will certainly subdue one single man in his shirt. But I have done; for those who have used to cramp liberty, have gone so far as to resent even the liberty of complaining; although a man upon the rack was never known to be refused the liberty of roaring as loud as he thought fit.

And as we are apt to sink too much under unreasonable fears, so we are too soon inclined to be raised by groundless hopes, according to the nature of all consumptive bodies like ours. Thus it has been given about, for several days

[1] William Molyneux (1656-1698), the philosopher and champion of Irish legislative independence in his 'Case of Ireland's being bound by Acts of Parliament in England,' 1698.

past, that somebody in England empowered a second somebody, to write to a third somebody here, to assure us that we should no more be troubled with these halfpence. And this is reported to have been done by the same person, who is said to have sworn some months ago, 'that he would ram them down our throats,' though I doubt they would stick in our stomachs; but whichever of these reports be true or false, it is no concern of ours. For, in this point, we have nothing to do with English ministers; and I should be sorry to leave it in their power to redress this grievance, or to enforce it; for the report of the Committee has given me a surfeit. The remedy is wholly in your own hands; and therefore I have digressed a little, in order to refresh and continue that spirit so seasonably raised among you; and to let you see, that by the laws of GOD, of NATURE, of NATIONS, and of your COUNTRY, you ARE, and OUGHT to be, as FREE a people as your brethren in England.

If the pamphlets published at London by Wood and his journeymen, in defence of his cause, were reprinted here, and our countrymen could be persuaded to read them, they would convince you of his wicked design more than all I shall ever be able to say. In short,

I make him a perfect saint in comparison of what he appears to be from the writings of those whom he hires to justify his project. But he is so far master of the field (let others guess the reason) that no London printer dare publish any paper written in favour of Ireland; and here nobody as yet has been so bold as to publish anything in favour of him.

There was, a few days ago, a pamphlet sent me, of near fifty pages, written in favour of Mr Wood and his coinage, printed in London; it is not worth answering, because probably it will never be published here. But it gave me occasion to reflect upon an unhappiness we lie under, that the people of England are utterly ignorant of our case; which, however, is no wonder, since it is a point they do not in the least concern themselves about, further than perhaps as a subject of discourse in a coffee-house, when they have nothing else to talk of. For I have reason to believe, that no minister ever gave himself the trouble of reading any papers written in our defence, because I suppose their opinions are already determined, and are formed wholly upon the reports of Wood and his accomplices; else it would be impossible that any man could have the impudence to write such a pamphlet as I have mentioned.

Our neighbours, whose understandings are just upon a level with ours (which perhaps are none of the brightest), have a strong contempt for most nations, but especially for Ireland. They look upon us as a sort of savage Irish, whom our ancestors conquered several hundred years ago. And if I should describe the Britons to you as they were in Cæsar's time, when they painted their bodies, or clothed themselves with the skins of beasts, I should act full as reasonably as they do. However, they are so far to be excused in relation to the present subject, that hearing only one side of the cause, and having neither opportunity nor curiosity to examine the other, they believe a lie merely for their ease; and conclude, because Mr Wood pretends to power he has also reason on his side.

Therefore, to let you see how this case is represented in England by Wood and his adherents, I have thought it proper to extract out of that pamphlet a few of those notorious falsehoods, in point of fact and reasoning, contained therein; the knowledge whereof will confirm my countrymen in their own right sentiments, when they will see, by comparing both, how much their enemies are in the wrong.

First, the writer positively asserts, 'that Wood's halfpence were current among us for several months, with the universal approbation of all people, without one single gainsayer; and we all, to a man, thought ourselves happy in having them.'

Secondly, he affirms, 'that we were drawn into dislike of them only by some cunning, evil-designing men among us, who opposed this patent of Wood to get another for themselves.'

Thirdly, 'that those who most declared at first against Wood's patent, were the very men who intend to get another for their own advantage.'

Fourthly, 'that our Parliament and Privy-council, the Lord Mayor and aldermen of Dublin, the grand juries and merchants, and, in short, the whole kingdom, nay, the very dogs,' as he expresses it, 'were fond of those halfpence, till they were inflamed by those few designing persons aforesaid.'

Fifthly, he says directly, 'that all those who opposed the halfpence, were Papists, and enemies to King George.'

Thus far, I am confident, the most ignorant among you can safely swear, from your own knowledge, that the author is a most notorious liar in every article; the direct contrary being so manifest to the whole kingdom, that, if occasion required, we might get it confirmed under five hundred thousand hands.

Sixthly, he would persuade us, 'that if we sell five shillings worth of our goods or manufactures for two shillings and fourpence worth of copper, although the copper were melted down, and that we could get five shillings in gold and silver for the said goods; yet to take the said two shillings and fourpence in copper, would be greatly for our advantage.'

And, lastly, he makes us a very fair offer, as empowered by Wood, 'that if we will take off two hundred thousand pounds in his halfpence for our goods, and likewise pay him three per cent. interest for thirty years for a hundred and twenty thousand pounds (at which he computes the coinage above the intrinsic value of the copper) for the loan of his coin, he will after that time give us good money for what halfpence will be then left.'

Let me place this offer in as clear a light as I can, to show the insupportable villainy and impudence of that incorrigible wretch. 'First,' says he, 'I will send two hundred thousand pounds of my coin into your country; the copper I compute to be, in real value, eighty thousand pounds, and I charge you with a hundred and twenty thousand pounds for the coinage; so that, you see, I lend you a hundred and twenty thousand pounds for thirty years; for which you shall pay me three per cent., that is to say, three thousand six hundred pounds per annum, which in thirty years will amount to a hundred and eight thousand pounds. And when these thirty years are expired, return me my copper, and I will give you good money for it.'

This is the proposal made to us by Wood in that pamphlet, written by one of his commissioners: and the author is supposed to be the same infamous Coleby, one of his under-swearers at the committee of council, who was tried for robbing the treasury here, where he was an under-clerk.

By this proposal, he will, first, receive two hundred thousand pounds in goods or sterling, for as much copper as he values at eighty thousand pounds, but in reality not worth thirty thousand pounds. Secondly, he will receive for interest a hundred and eight thousand pounds: and when our children come thirty years hence to return his halfpence upon his executors (for before that time he will be probably gone to his own place) those executors will very reasonably reject them as raps and counterfeits, which they will be, and millions of them of his own coinage.

Methinks I am fond of such a dealer as this, who mends every day upon our hands, like a Dutch reckoning; wherein if you dispute the unreasonableness and exorbitance of the bill, the landlord shall bring it up every time with new additions.

Although these, and the like pamphlets, published by Wood in London, are altogether unknown here, where nobody could read them without as much indignation as contempt would allow; yet I thought it proper to give you a specimen how the man employs his time, where he rides alone without any creature to contradict him; while our FEW FRIENDS there wonder at our silence: and the English in general, if they think of this matter at all, impute our refusal to wilfulness or disaffection, just as Wood and his hirelings are pleased to represent.

But although our arguments are not suffered to be printed in England, yet the consequence will be of little moment. Let Wood endeavour to persuade the people there, that we ought to receive his coin; and let me convince our people here, that they ought to reject it, under pain of our utter undoing; and then let him do his best and his worst.

Before I conclude, I must beg leave, in all humility, to tell Mr Wood, that he is guilty of great indiscretion, by causing so honourable a name as that of Mr Walpole to be mentioned so often, and in such a manner, upon this occasion. A short paper printed at Bristol, and reprinted here, reports Mr Wood to say, 'that he wonders at the impudence and insolence of the Irish in refusing his coin, and what he will do when Mr Walpole comes to town.' Where, by the way, he is mistaken; for it is the true English people of Ireland who refuse it, although we take it for granted that the Irish will do so too whenever they are asked. In another printed paper of his contriving, it is roundly expressed, 'that Mr Walpole will cram his brass down our throats.' Sometimes it is given out, 'that we must either take those halfpence, or eat our brogues:' and in another newsletter, but of yesterday, we read, 'that the same great man has sworn to make us swallow his coin in fireballs.'

This brings to my mind the known story of a Scotchman, who, receiving the sentence of death with all the circumstances of hanging, beheading, quartering, embowelling, and the like, cried out, 'What need all this COOKERY?' And I think we have reason to ask the same question; for, if we believe Wood, here is a dinner ready for us; and you see the bill of fare; and I am sorry the drink was forgot, which might easily be supplied with melted lead and flaming pitch.

What vile words are these to put into the mouth of a great counsellor, in high trust with his majesty, and looked upon as a prime-minister? If Mr Wood has no better a manner of representing his patrons, when I come to be a great man he shall never be suffered to attend at my levee. This is not the style of a great minister; it savours too much of the kettle and the furnace, and came entirely out of Wood's forge.

As for the threat of making us eat our brogues, we need not be in pain; for, if his coin should pass, that unpolite covering for the feet would no longer be a national reproach; because then we should have neither shoe nor brogue left in the kingdom. But here the falsehood of Mr Wood is fairly detected; for I am confident Mr Walpole never heard of a brogue in his whole life.

As to 'swallowing these halfpence in fire-balls,' it is a story equally improbable. For, to execute this operation, the whole stock of Mr Wood's coin and metal must be melted down, and moulded into hollow balls with wild-fire, no bigger than a reasonable throat may be able to swallow. Now, the metal he has prepared, and already coined, will amount to at least fifty millions of halfpence, to be swallowed by a million and a half of people: so that, allowing two halfpence to each ball, there will be about seventeen balls of wild-fire a-piece to be swallowed by every person in the kingdom; and to administer this dose, there cannot be conveniently fewer than fifty thousand operators, allowing one operator to every thirty; which, considering the squeamishness of some stomachs, and the peevishness of young children, is but reasonable. Now, under correction of better judgments, I think the trouble and charge of such an experiment would exceed the profit; and therefore I take this report to be spurious, or, at least, only a new scheme of Mr Wood himself; which, to make it pass the better in Ireland, he would father upon a minister of state.

But I will now demonstrate, beyond all contradiction, that Mr Walpole is against this project of Mr Wood, and is an entire friend to Ireland, only by this one invincible argument; that he has the universal opinion of being a wise man, an able minister, and in all his proceedings pursuing the true interest of the King his master; and that as his integrity is above all corruption, so is his fortune above all temptation. I reckon, therefore, we are perfectly safe from that corner, and shall never be under the necessity of contending with so formidable a power, but be left to possess our brogues and potatoes in peace, as remote from thunder as we are from Jupiter.

  I am, my dear countrymen,
   Your loving fellow-subject,
    Fellow-sufferer, and humble servant,
          M. B.

IX

LETTERS OF JUNIUS

[There is no need to enter here on the vexed question as to who Junius was, except so far as to say that the claims of Sir Philip Francis are open to fewer objections than those of any of his numerous competitors, and have been generally recognised. The three following letters were written in 1769; Chatham had been compelled to retire from his own ministry and leave the premiership to the Duke of Grafton, whose administration showed every sign of incompetence and failure. The difficulties with America were growing acute owing to its blunders; popular discontent at home was fanned by the monstrous attempt to keep Wilkes out of Parliament, and corruption in politics had reached an unprecedented height. At the same time the attempt of the king to govern as well as reign roused the suspicions and fears of the people in general. The first letter reprinted is the first of Junius's letters, and is general in its scope and character, describing the evils of the time. His later letters are usually attacks on some particular person.][1]

---

[1] See Introd., p. 21.

LETTER I

TO THE PRINTER OF THE PUBLIC ADVERTISER

21 *January* 1769.

SIR,—The submission of a free people to the executive authority of government is no more than a compliance with laws, which they themselves have enacted. While the national honour is firmly maintained abroad, and while justice is impartially administered at home, the obedience of the subject will be voluntary, cheerful, and I might almost say, unlimited. A generous nation is grateful even for the preservation of its rights, and willingly extends the respect due to the office of a good prince into an affection for his person. Loyalty, in the heart and understanding of an Englishman, is a rational attachment to the guardian of the laws. Prejudices and passion have sometimes carried it to a criminal length; and, whatever foreigners may imagine, we know that Englishmen have erred as much in a mistaken zeal for particular persons and families, as they ever did in defence of what they thought most dear and interesting to themselves.

It naturally fills us with resentment, to see

such a temper insulted, or abused. In reading the history of a free people, whose rights have been invaded, we are interested in their cause. Our own feelings tell us how long they ought to have submitted, and at what moment it would have been treachery to themselves not to have resisted. How much warmer will be our resentment, if experience should bring the fatal example home to ourselves!

The situation of this country is alarming enough to rouse the attention of every man, who pretends to a concern for the public welfare. Appearances justify suspicion; and, when the safety of a nation is at stake, suspicion is a just ground of enquiry. Let us enter into it with candour and decency. Respect is due to the station of ministers; and, if a resolution must at last be taken, there is none so likely to be supported with firmness, as that which has been adopted with moderation.

The ruin or prosperity of a state depends so much upon the administration of its government, that, to be acquainted with the merit of a ministry, we need only observe the condition of the people. If we see them obedient to the laws, prosperous in their industry, united at home, and respected abroad, we may reasonably presume that their affairs are conducted by men of experience, abilities, and virtue. If, on the contrary, we see a universal spirit of distrust and dissatisfaction, a rapid decay of trade, dissensions in all parts of the empire, and a total loss of respect in the eyes of foreign powers, we may pronounce, without hesitation, that the government of that country is weak, distracted, and corrupt. The multitude, in all countries, are patient to a certain point. Ill-usage may rouse their indignation, and hurry them into excesses, but the original fault is in government.[1] Perhaps there never was an instance of a change, in the circumstances and temper of a whole nation, so sudden and extraordinary as that which the misconduct of ministers has, within these very few years, produced in Great Britain. When our gracious Sovereign ascended the throne, we were a flourishing and a contented people. If the personal virtues of a king could have insured the happiness of his subjects, the scene could not have altered so entirely as it has done. The idea of uniting all parties, of trying all characters, and of distributing the offices of state by rotation, was gracious and benevolent to an extreme, though it has not yet produced

---

[1] Compare p. 287, where Burke makes some very similar reflections.

the many salutary effects which were intended by it. To say nothing of the wisdom of such a plan, it undoubtedly arose from an unbounded goodness of heart, in which folly had no share. It was not a capricious partiality to new faces:— it was not a natural turn for low intrigue; nor was it the treacherous amusement of double and triple negotiations. No, Sir, it arose from a continued anxiety, in the purest of all possible hearts, for the general welfare. Unfortunately for us, the event has not been answerable to the design. After a rapid succession of changes, we are reduced to that state, which hardly any change can mend. Yet there is no extremity of distress, which of itself ought to reduce a great nation to despair. It is not the disorder, but the physician;—it is not a casual concurrence of calamitous circumstances, it is the pernicious hand of government, which alone can make a whole people desperate.

Without much political sagacity, or any extraordinary depth of observation, we need only mark how the principal departments of the state are bestowed, and look no farther for the true cause of every mischief that befalls us.

The finances of a nation, sinking under its debts and expenses, are committed to a young nobleman already ruined by play.[1] Introduced to act under the auspices of lord Chatham, and left at the head of affairs by that nobleman's retreat, he became minister by accident; but deserting the principles and professions which gave him a moment's popularity, we see him, from every honourable engagement to the public, an apostate by design. As for business, the world yet knows nothing of his talents or resolution; unless a wayward, wavering inconsistency be a mark of genius, and caprice a demonstration of spirit. It may be said perhaps, that it is his Grace's province, as surely it is his passion, rather to distribute than to save the public money, and that while lord North is chancellor of the Exchequer, the first lord of the Treasury may be as thoughtless and as extravagant as he pleases. I hope, however, he will not rely too much on the fertility of lord North's genius for finance. His Lordship is yet to give us the first proof of his abilities: It may be candid to suppose that he has hitherto voluntarily concealed his talents; intending perhaps to astonish the world, when we least expect it, with a knowledge of trade, a choice of expedients, and a depth of resources equal

[1] The Duke of Grafton.

to the necessities, and far beyond the hopes, of his country. He must now exert the whole power of his capacity, if he would wish us to forget, that, since he has been in office, no plan has been formed, no system adhered to, nor any one important measure adopted for the relief of public credit. If his plan for the service of the current year be not irrevocably fixed on, let me warn him to think seriously of consequences before he ventures to increase the public debt. Outraged and oppressed as we are, this nation will not bear, after a six years' peace, to see new millions borrowed, without an eventual diminution of debt, or reduction of interest. The attempt might rouse a spirit of resentment, which might reach beyond the sacrifice of a minister. As to the debt upon the civil list, the people of England expect that it will not be paid without a strict enquiry how it was incurred. If it must be paid by parliament, let me advise the chancellor of the Exchequer to think of some better expedient than a lottery. To support an expensive war, or in circumstances of absolute necessity, a lottery may perhaps be allowable; but, besides that it is at all times the very worst way of raising money upon the people,

I think it ill becomes the royal dignity to have the debts of a king provided for, like the repairs of a country bridge, or a decayed hospital. The management of the king's affairs in the House of Commons cannot be more disgraced that it has been. A leading minister[1] repeatedly called down for absolute ignorance;—ridiculous motions ridiculously withdrawn;—deliberate plans disconcerted, and a week's preparation of graceful oratory lost in a moment, give us some, though not an adequate, idea of lord North's parliamentary abilities and influence. Yet before he had the misfortune to be chancellor of the Exchequer, he was neither an object of derision to his enemies, nor of melancholy pity to his friends.

A series of inconsistent measures had alienated the colonies from their duty as subjects, and from their natural affection to their common country. When Mr Grenville was placed at the head of the Treasury, he felt the impossibility of Great Britain's supporting such an establishment as her former successes had made indispensable, and at the same time of giving any sensible relief to foreign trade, and to the weight of the public debt. He thought

[1] Lord North.

it equitable that those parts of the empire, which had benefitted most by the expenses of the war, should contribute something to the expenses of the peace, and he had no doubt of the constitutional right vested in parliament to raise that contribution. But, unfortunately for this country, Mr Grenville was at any rate to be distressed, because he was minister, and Mr Pitt and lord Camden were to be the patrons of America, because they were in opposition. Their declarations gave spirit and argument to the colonies, and while perhaps they meant no more than the ruin of a minister, they in effect divided one half of the empire from the other.

Under one administration the Stamp Act is made; under the second it is repealed; under the third, in spite of all experience, a new mode of taxing the colonies is invented, and a question revived, which ought to have been buried in oblivion. In these circumstances a new office is established for the business of the plantations, and the earl of Hillsborough called forth, at a most critical season, to govern America. The choice at least announced to us a man of superior capacity and knowledge. Whether he be so or not, let his despatches, as far as they have appeared, let his measures as far as they have operated, determine for him. In the former we have seen strong assertions without proof, declamation without argument, and violent censures without dignity or moderation; but neither correctness in the composition, nor judgment in the design. As for his measures, let it be remembered, that he was called upon to conciliate and unite; and that, when he entered into office, the most refractory of the colonies were still disposed to proceed by the constitutional methods of petition and remonstrance. Since that period they have been driven into excesses little short of rebellion. Petitions have been hindered from reaching the throne; and the continuance of one of the principal assemblies rested upon an arbitrary condition, which, considering the temper they were in, it was impossible they should comply with, and which would have availed nothing as to the general question, if it had been complied with. So violent, and I believe I may call it so unconstitutional, an exertion of the prerogative, to say nothing of the weak, injudicious terms in which it was conveyed, gives us as humble an opinion of his Lordship's capacity, as it does of his temper and moderation. While we are at peace with other nations, our military force may perhaps be spared to support the earl of Hillsborough's measures in America. Whenever that force shall be necessarily withdrawn or diminished, the dismission of such a minister will neither console us for his imprudence, nor remove the settled resentment of a people, who, complaining of an act of the legislature, are outraged by an unwarrantable stretch of prerogative, and supporting their claims by argument, are insulted with declamation.

Drawing lots would be a prudent and reasonable method of appointing the officers of state, compared to a late disposition of the secretary's office. Lord Rochford was acquainted with the affairs and temper of the southern courts: lord Weymouth was equally qualified for either department. By what unaccountable caprice has it happened, that the latter, who pretends to no experience whatsoever, is removed to the most important of the two departments, and the former by preference placed in an office, where his experience can be of no use to him? lord Weymouth had distinguished himself in his first employment by a spirited, if not judicious conduct. He had animated the civil magistrate beyond the tone of civil authority, and had directed the operations of the army to more than military execution. Recovered from the errors of his youth, from the distraction of play, and the bewitching smiles of Burgundy, behold him exerting the whole strength of his clear, unclouded faculties, in the service of the crown. It was not the heat of midnight excesses, nor ignorance of the laws, nor the furious spirit of the house of Bedford: No, Sir, when this respectable minister interposed his authority between the magistrate and the people, and signed the mandate, on which, for aught he knew, the lives of thousands depended, he did it from the deliberate motion of his heart, supported by the best of his judgment.[1]

It has lately been a fashion to pay a compliment to the bravery and generosity of the commander-in-chief,[2] at the expense of his understanding. They who love him least

---

[1] During the riots connected with Wilkes's election in 1768, Weymouth wrote urging the magistrates not to scruple to employ soldiers against the people; cf. p. 320. It should be remembered that hitherto there had been only two secretaries of state, for the northern and southern departments. The former had charge of home affairs. In 1768 lord Hillsborough became first secretary of state for the colonies, thus bringing the number up to three.

[2] Lord Granby.

make no question of his courage, while his friends dwell chiefly on the facility of his disposition. Admitting him to be as brave as a total absence of all feeling and reflection can make him, let us see what sort of merit he derives from the remainder of his character. If it be generosity to accumulate in his own person and family a number of lucrative employments; to provide, at the public expense, for every creature that bears the name of Manners; and, neglecting the merit and services of the rest of the army, to heap promotions upon his favourites and dependants, the present commander-in-chief is the most generous man alive. Nature has been sparing of her gifts to this noble lord; but where birth and fortune are united, we expect the noble pride and independence of a man of spirit, not the servile, humiliating compliances of a courtier. As to the goodness of his heart, if a proof of it be taken from the facility of never refusing, what conclusion shall we draw from the independency of never performing? And if the discipline of the army be in any degree preserved, what thanks are due to a man, whose cares, notoriously confined to filling up vacancies, have degraded the office of commander-in-chief into a broker of commissions?

With respect to the navy, I shall only say, that this country is so highly indebted to sir Edward Hawke, that no expense should be spared to secure to him an honourable and affluent retreat.

The pure and impartial administration of justice is perhaps the firmest bond to secure a cheerful submission of the people, and to engage their affections to government. It is not sufficient that questions of private right and wrong are justly decided, nor that judges are superior to the vileness of pecuniary corruption. Jefferies himself, when the court had no interest, was an upright judge. A court of justice may be subject to another sort of bias, more important and pernicious, as it reaches beyond the interest of individuals, and affects the whole community. A judge under the influence of government, may be honest enough in the decision of private causes, yet a traitor to the public. When a victim is marked out by the ministry, this judge will offer himself to perform the sacrifice. He will not scruple to prostitute his dignity, and betray the sanctity of his office, whenever an arbitrary point is to be carried for government, or the resentments of a court are to be gratified.

These principles and proceedings, odious and contemptible as they are, in effect are no less injudicious. A wise and generous people are roused by every appearance of oppressive, unconstitutional measures, whether those measures are supported openly by the power of government, or masked under the forms of a court of justice. Prudence and self-preservation will oblige the most moderate dispositions to make common cause, even with a man whose conduct they censure, if they see him persecuted in a way which the real spirit of the laws will not justify. The facts, on which these remarks are founded, are too notorious to require an application.

This, Sir, is the detail. In one view behold a nation overwhelmed with debt; her revenues wasted; her trade declining; the affections of her colonies alienated; the duty of the magistrate transferred to the soldiery; a gallant army, which never fought unwillingly but against their fellow-subjects, mouldering away for want of the direction of a man of common abilities and spirit; and, in the last instance, the administration of justice become odious and suspected to the whole body of the people. This deplorable scene admits but of one addition — that we are governed by counsels, from which a reasonable man can expect no remedy but poison, no relief but death.

If, by the immediate interposition of Providence, it were possible for us to escape a crisis so full of terror and despair, posterity will not believe the history of the present times. They will either conclude that our distresses were imaginary, or that we had the good fortune to be governed by men of acknowledged integrity and wisdom: they will not believe it possible that their ancestors could have survived, or recovered from so desperate a condition, while a duke of Grafton was prime minister, a lord North chancellor of the Exchequer, a Weymouth and a Hillsborough secretaries of state, a Granby commander-in-chief, and a Mansfield chief criminal judge of the kingdom.

JUNIUS.

X

LETTERS OF JUNIUS

[This letter is an attack on John Russell, fourth Duke of Bedford (1710-1771), the head of the 'Bloomsbury gang,' as his adherents were called. They were of sufficient strength to constitute if not a party at any rate a faction by themselves. Bedford's character and career do not merit much admiration but they were far different from what Junius represents them to be. This letter is indeed one of the most effective but certainly one of the most venomous attacks on a politician to be found in the whole range of English political literature. For an exhaustive examination of Junius's insinuations and falsehoods the reader is referred to Brougham's Statesmen of George III.' and Lord John Russell's introduction to the third volume of the 'Bedford Correspondence.']

LETTER XXIII

TO
HIS GRACE THE DUKE OF BEDFORD

19 *Sept.* 1769.

My Lord,—You are so little accustomed to receive any marks of respect or esteem from the public that if, in the following lines, a compliment or expression of applause should escape me, I fear you would consider it as a mockery of your established character, and perhaps an insult to your understanding. You have nice feelings, my Lord, if we may judge from your resentments. Cautious therefore of giving offence, where you have so little deserved it, I shall leave the illustration of your virtues to other hands. Your friends have a privilege to play upon the easiness of your temper, or possibly they are better acquainted with your good qualities than I am. You have done good by stealth. The rest is upon record. You have still left ample room for speculation, when panegyric is exhausted.

You are indeed a very considerable man. The highest rank; a splendid fortune; and a name, glorious till it was yours, were sufficient to have supported you with meaner abilities than I think you possess. From the first you derived a constitutional claim to respect; from the second, a natural extensive authority;—the last created a partial expectation of hereditary virtues. The use you have made of these uncommon advantages might have been more honourable to yourself, but could not be more instructive to mankind. We may trace it in the veneration of your country, the choice of your friends, and in the accomplishment of every sanguine hope, which the public might have conceived from the illustrious name of Russell.

The eminence of your station gave you a commanding prospect of your duty. The road which led to honour, was open to your view. You could not lose it by mistake, and you had no temptation to depart from it by design. Compare the natural dignity and importance of the richest peer of England;—the noble independence which he might have maintained in parliament, and the real interest and respect which he might have acquired, not only in parliament, but through the whole kingdom; compare these glorious distinctions with the ambition of holding a share in government, the emoluments of a place, the sale of a borough, or the purchase of a corporation; and though you may not regret the virtues which create respect, you may see with anguish how much real importance and authority you have lost. Consider the character of an independent virtuous duke of Bedford; imagine what he might be in this country, then reflect one moment upon what you are. If it be possible for me to withdraw my attention from the fact, I will tell you in theory what such a man might be.

Conscious of his own weight and importance, his conduct in parliament would be directed by nothing but the constitutional duty of a peer. He would consider himself as a guardian of the laws. Willing to support the just measures of government, but determined to observe the conduct of the minister with suspicion, he would oppose the violence of faction with as much firmness as the encroachments of prerogative. He would be as little capable of bargaining with the minister for places for himself, or his dependents, as of descending to mix himself in the intrigues of opposition. Whenever an important question called for his opinion in parliament, he would be heard, by the most profligate minister, with deference and respect. His authority would either sanctify or disgrace the measures of government.—The people would look up to him as to their protector, and a virtuous prince would have one honest man in his dominions, in whose integrity and judgment he might safely confide. If it should be the will of Providence to afflict him with a domestic misfortune, he would submit to the stroke with feeling, but not without dignity. He would consider the people as his children, and receive a generous heartfelt consolation, in the sympathizing tears and blessings of his country.

Your Grace may probably discover something more intelligible in the negative part of this illustrious character. The man I have described would never prostitute his dignity in parliament by an indecent violence either in opposing or defending a minister. He would not at one moment rancorously persecute, at another basely cringe to, the favourite of his sovereign. After outraging the royal dignity with peremptory conditions, little short of menace and hostility, he would never descend to the humility of soliciting an interview with the favourite, and of offering to recover, at any price, the honour of his friendship. Though deceived perhaps in his youth, he would not, through the course of a long life, have invariably chosen his friends from among the most profligate of mankind. His own honour would have forbidden him from mixing his private pleasures or conversation with jockeys, gamesters, blasphemers, gladiators, or buffoons. He would then have never felt, much less would he have submitted to the humiliating, dishonest necessity of engaging in the interest and intrigues of his dependents, of supplying their vices, or relieving their beggary, at the expense of his country. He would not have betrayed such ignorance, or such contempt of the constitution, as openly to avow, in a court of justice, the purchase and sale of a borough. He would not have thought it consistent with his rank in the state, or even with his personal importance, to be the little tyrant of a little corporation. He would never have been insulted with virtues, which he had laboured to extinguish, nor suffered the disgrace of a mortifying defeat, which has made him ridiculous and contemptible, even to the few by whom he was not detested.—I reverence the afflictions of a good man,—his sorrows are sacred. But how can we take part in the distresses of a man, whom we can neither love nor esteem; or feel for a calamity of which he himself is insensible? Where was the father's heart when he could look for or find an immediate consolation for the loss of an only son, in consultations and bargains for a place at court, and even in the misery of balloting at the India House!

Admitting then that you have mistaken or deserted those honourable principles, which ought to have directed your conduct; admitting that you have as little claim to private affection as to public esteem, let us see with what abilities, with what degree of judgment, you have carried your own system into execution. A great man, in the success and even in the magnitude of his crimes, finds a rescue from contempt. Your Grace is every way unfortunate. Yet I will not look back to those ridiculous scenes, by which in your earlier days you thought it an honour to be distinguished; the recorded stripes, the public infamy, your own sufferings, or Mr Rigby's fortitude.[1] These events undoubtedly left an impression, though not upon your mind. To *such* a mind, it may perhaps be a pleasure to reflect, that there is hardly a corner of any of his Majesty's kingdoms, except France, in which, at one time or other, your valuable life has not been in danger. Amiable man! we see and acknowledge the protection of Providence, by which you have so often escaped the personal detestation of your fellow-subjects, and are still reserved for the public justice of your country.

Your history begins to be important at that auspicious period at which you were deputed to represent the earl of Bute, at the court of Versailles. It was an honourable office, and executed with the same spirit

---

[1] In 1752 Richard Rigby (1722-1788) rescued the duke from the violence of the mob at the Lichfield races.

with which it was accepted. Your patrons wanted an ambassador, who would submit to make concessions, without daring to insist upon any honourable condition for his sovereign. Their business required a man, who had as little feeling for his own dignity as for the welfare of his country; and they found him in the first rank of the nobility. Belleisle, Goree, Guadaloupe, St Lucia, Martinique, the Fishery,[1] and the Havanna, are glorious monuments of your Grace's talents for negotiation. My Lord, we are too well acquainted with your pecuniary character, to think it possible that so many public sacrifices should have been made, without some private compensations. Your conduct carries with it an internal evidence, beyond all the legal proofs of a court of justice. Even the callous pride of lord Egremont was alarmed. He saw and felt his own dishonour in corresponding with you; and there certainly was a moment, at which he meant to have resisted, had not a fatal lethargy prevailed over his faculties, and carried all sense and memory away with it.

I will not pretend to specify the secret terms on which you were invited to support an ad-

---

[1] *I.e.* off Newfoundland; all these acquisitions were given up by the peace of Paris in 1763.

ministration which lord Bute pretended to leave in full possession of their ministerial authority, and perfectly masters of themselves. He was not of a temper to relinquish power, though he retired from employment. Stipulations were certainly made between your Grace and him, and certainly violated. After two years' submission, you thought you had collected a strength sufficient to controul his influence, and that it was your turn to be a tyrant, because you had been a slave. When you found yourself mistaken in your opinion of your gracious Master's firmness, disappointment got the better of all your humble discretion, and carried you to an excess of outrage to his person, as distant from true spirit, as from all decency and respect. After robbing him of the rights of a king, you would not permit him to preserve the honour of a gentleman. It was then lord Weymouth was nominated to Ireland, and despatched (we well remember with what indecent hurry) to plunder the treasury of the first fruits of an employment which you well knew he was never to execute.

This sudden declaration of war against the favourite might have given you a momentary merit with the public, if it had either been adopted upon principle, or maintained with resolution. Without looking back to all your former servility, we need only observe your subsequent conduct, to see upon what motives you acted. Apparently united with Mr Grenville, you waited until lord Rockingham's feeble administration should dissolve in its own weakness.—The moment their dismission was suspected, the moment you perceived that another system was adopted in the closet, you thought it no disgrace to return to your former dependence, and solicit once more the friendship of lord Bute. You begged an interview, at which he had spirit enough to treat you with contempt.

It would now be of little use to point out, by what a train of weak, injudicious measures it became necessary, or was thought so, to call you back to a share in the administration. The friends, whom you did not in the last instance desert, were not of a character to add strength or credit to government; and at that time your alliance with the duke of Grafton was, I presume, hardly foreseen. We must look for other stipulations, to account for that sudden resolution of the closet, by which three of your dependants (whose characters, I think, cannot be less respected than they are) were advanced to offices, through which you might again controul the minister, and probably engross the whole direction of affairs.

The possession of absolute power is now once more within your reach. The measures you have taken to obtain and confirm it, are too gross to escape the eyes of a discerning judicious prince. His palace is besieged; the lines of circumvallation are drawing round him; and unless he finds a resource in his own activity, or in the attachment of the real friends of his family, the best of princes must submit to the confinement of a state prisoner, until your Grace's death, or some less fortunate event, shall raise the siege. For the present, you may safely resume that style of insult and menace, which even a private gentleman cannot submit to hear without being contemptible. Mr Mackenzie's history is not yet forgotten, and you may find precedents enough of the mode, in which an imperious subject may signify his pleasure to his sovereign. Where will this gracious monarch look for assistance, when the wretched Grafton could forget his obligations to his master, and desert him for a hollow alliance with *such* a man as the duke of Bedford!

Let us consider you, then, as arrived at the summit of worldly greatness; let us suppose, that all your plans of avarice and ambition are accomplished, and your most sanguine wishes gratified in the fear as well as the hatred of the people: Can age itself forget that you are now in the last act of life? Can grey hairs make folly venerable? and is there no period to be reserved for meditation and retirement? For shame! my Lord: let it not be recorded of you, that the latest moments of your life were dedicated to the same unworthy pursuits, the same busy agitations, in which your youth and manhood were exhausted. Consider, that, although you cannot disgrace your former life, you are violating the character of age, and exposing the impotent imbecility, after you have lost the vigour of the passions.

Your friends will ask, perhaps, Whither shall this unhappy old man retire? Can he remain in the metropolis, where his life has been so often threatened, and his palace so often attacked? If he returns to Woburn, scorn and mockery await him. He must create a solitude round his estate, if he would avoid the face of reproach and derision. At Plymouth, his destruction would be more than probable; at Exeter, inevitable. No honest Englishman will ever forget his attachment, nor any honest Scotchman forgive his treachery, to lord Bute. At every town he enters, he must change his liveries and his name. Which ever way he flies, the *Hue and Cry* of the country pursues him.

In another kingdom, indeed, the blessings of his administration have been more sensibly felt; his virtues better understood; or at worst, they will not, for him alone, forget their hospitality. — As well might VERRES have returned to Sicily. You have twice escaped, my Lord; beware of a third experiment. The indignation of a whole people, plundered, insulted, and oppressed as they have been, will not always be disappointed.

It is in vain therefore to shift the scene. You can no more fly from your enemies than from yourself. Persecuted abroad, you look into your own heart for consolation, and find nothing but reproaches and despair. But, my Lord, you may quit the field of business, though not the field of danger; and though you cannot be safe, you may cease to be ridiculous. I fear you have listened too long to the advice of those pernicious friends, with whose interests you have sordidly united your own, and for whom you have sacrificed every thing that ought to be dear to a man of honour. They are still base enough to encourage the follies of your age, as they once did the vices of your youth. As little acquainted with the rules of decorum, as with the laws of morality, they will not suffer you to profit by experience, nor even to consult the propriety of a bad character. Even now they tell you, that life is no more than a dramatic scene, in which the hero should preserve his consistency to the last, and that as you lived without virtue, you should die without repentance.

XI

LETTERS OF JUNIUS

[The excitement caused by these letters culminated in the following addressed to the king, whom Junius hated even more than he hated his ministers. This letter is perhaps unique in its outspokenness, but unlike most of Junius's letters there is little that is actually scurrilous in it except the ferocious attack on the Scots.][1]

LETTER XXXV

FOR THE PUBLIC ADVERTISER

19 December, 1769.

WHEN the complaints of a brave and powerful people are observed to increase in proportion to the wrongs they have suffered; when, instead of sinking into submission, they are roused to resistance, the time will soon arrive at which every inferior consideration must yield to the security of the sovereign, and to the general safety of the state. There is a moment of difficulty and danger, at which flattery and falsehood can no longer deceive, and simplicity itself

---

[1] See Lecky's *Hist. of England*, ed. 1892, iii. 446, 399.

can no longer be misled. Let us suppose it arrived. Let us suppose a gracious, well-intentioned Prince, made sensible at last of the great duty he owes to his people, and of his own disgraceful situation; that he looks round him for assistance, and asks for no advice, but how to gratify the wishes and secure the happiness of his subjects. In these circumstances, it may be matter of curious SPECULATION to consider, if an honest man were permitted to approach a king, in what terms he would address himself to his sovereign. Let it be imagined, no matter how improbable, that the first prejudice against his character is removed, that the ceremonious difficulties of an audience are surmounted, that he feels himself animated by the purest and most honourable affections to his king and country, and that the great person, whom he addresses, has spirit enough to bid him speak freely, and understanding enough to listen to him with attention. Unacquainted with the vain impertinence of forms, he would deliver his sentiments with dignity and firmness, but not without respect.

SIR,—It is the misfortune of your life, and originally the cause of every reproach and distress which has attended your government, that you should never have been acquainted with the language of truth, until you heard it in the complaints of your people. It is not, however, too late to correct the error of your education. We are still inclined to make an indulgent allowance for the pernicious lessons you received in your youth, and to form the most sanguine hopes from the natural benevolence of your disposition. We are far from thinking you capable of a direct, deliberate purpose to invade those original rights of your subjects, on which all their civil and political liberties depend. Had it been possible for us to entertain a suspicion so dishonourable to your character, we should long since have adopted a style of remonstrance very distant from the humility of complaint. The doctrine inculcated by our laws, *That the King can do no wrong*, is admitted without reluctance. We separate the amiable, good-natured prince from the folly and treachery of his servants, and the private virtues of the man from the vices of his government. Were it not for this just distinction, I know not whether your Majesty's condition, or that of the English nation, would deserve most to be lamented. I would prepare your mind for a favourable reception of truth, by removing every painful, offensive idea of personal reproach. Your subjects, Sir, wish for nothing but that, as *they* are reasonable and affectionate enough to separate your person from your government, so *you*, in your turn, should distinguish between the conduct which becomes the permanent dignity of a king, and that which serves only to promote the temporary interest and miserable ambition of a minister.

You ascended the throne with a declared, and, I doubt not, a sincere resolution of giving universal satisfaction to your subjects. You found them pleased with the novelty of a young prince, whose countenance promised even more than his words, and loyal to you not only from principle, but passion. It was not a cold profession of allegiance to the first magistrate, but a partial, animated attachment to a favourite prince, the native of their country. They did not wait to examine your conduct, nor to be determined by experience, but gave you a generous credit for the future blessings of your reign, and paid you in advance the dearest tribute of their affections. Such, Sir, was once the disposition of a people, who now surround your throne with reproaches and complaints. Do justice to yourself. Banish from your mind those unworthy opinions, with which some interested persons have laboured to possess you.

Distrust the men, who tell you that the English are naturally light and inconstant;—that they complain without a cause. Withdraw your confidence equally from all parties, from ministers, favourites, and relations; and let there be one moment in your life, in which you have consulted your own understanding.

When you affectedly renounced the name of Englishman,[1] believe me, Sir, you were persuaded to pay a very ill-judged compliment to one part of your subjects, at the expense of another. While the natives of Scotland are not in actual rebellion, they are undoubtedly entitled to protection; nor do I mean to condemn the policy of giving some encouragement to the novelty of their affections for the house of Hanover. I am ready to hope for every thing from their new-born zeal, and from the future steadiness of their allegiance. But hitherto they have no claim to your favour. To honour them with a determined predilection and confidence, in exclusion of your English subjects, who placed your family, and, in spite of treachery and rebellion, have supported it upon the throne, is a mistake too gross, even for the unsuspecting generosity of youth. In this error we see a capital violation of

---

[1] George III. gloried in the name of Briton.

the most obvious rules of policy and prudence. We trace it, however, to an original bias in your education, and are ready to allow for your inexperience.

To the same early influence we attribute it, that you have descended to take a share not only in the narrow views and interests of particular persons, but in the fatal malignity of their passions. At your accession to the throne, the whole system of government was altered, not from wisdom or deliberation, but because it had been adopted by your predecessor. A little personal motive of pique and resentment was sufficient to remove the ablest servants of the crown;[1] but it is not in this country, Sir, that such men can be dishonoured by the frowns of a king. They were dismissed, but could not be disgraced. Without entering into a minuter discussion of the merits of the peace,[2] we may observe, in the imprudent hurry with which the first overtures from France were accepted, in the conduct of the negotiation, and terms

---

[1] *E.g.* Henry Bilson Legge, Chancellor of the Exchequer, who was dismissed in March 1761 for refusing to support the candidature of Bute's friend Simeon Stuart for Parliament, and for refusing to move a motion for paying large sums to the landgrave of Hesse.

[2] The peace of Paris, Nov. 1762.

of the treaty, the strongest marks of that precipitate spirit of concession, with which a certain part of your subjects have been at all times ready to purchase a peace with the natural enemies of this country. On *your* part we are satisfied that every thing was honourable and sincere, and if England was sold to France, we doubt not that your Majesty was equally betrayed. The conditions of the peace were matter of grief and surprise to your subjects, but not the immediate cause of their present discontent.

Hitherto, Sir, you had been sacrificed to the prejudices and passions of others. With what firmness will you bear the mention of your own?

A man, not very honourably distinguished in the world, commences a formal attack upon your favourite, considering nothing, but how he might best expose his person and principles to detestation, and the national character of his countrymen to contempt. The natives of that country, Sir, are as much distinguished by a peculiar character, as by your Majesty's favour. Like another chosen people, they have been conducted into the land of plenty, where they find themselves effectually marked, and divided from mankind. There is hardly a period, at which the most irregular character may not be redeemed. The mistakes of one sex find a retreat in patriotism,[1] those of the other, in devotion. Mr Wilkes brought with him into politics the same liberal sentiments, by which his private conduct had been directed, and seemed to think, that, as there are few excesses in which an English gentleman may not be permitted to indulge, the same latitude was allowed him in the choice of his political principles, and in the spirit of maintaining them.—I mean to state, not entirely to defend his conduct. In the earnestness of his zeal, he suffered some unwarrantable insinuations to escape him. He said more than moderate men would justify; but not enough to entitle him to the honour of your Majesty's personal resentment. The rays of royal indignation, collected upon him, served only to illuminate, and could not consume. Animated by the favour of the people on one side, and heated by persecution on the other, his views and sentiments changed with his situation. Hardly serious at first, he is now an enthusiast. The coldest bodies warm with opposition, the hardest sparkle in collision. There is a holy mistaken zeal in politics as well as in religion.

[1] Compare Johnson's remark that 'patriotism was the last refuge of scoundrels.'

By persuading others, we convince ourselves. The passions are engaged, and create a maternal affection in the mind, which forces us to love the cause for which we suffer.—Is this a contention worthy of a king? Are you not sensible how much the meanness of the cause gives an air of ridicule to the serious difficulties into which you have been betrayed? the destruction of one man has been now, for many years, the sole object of your government; and if there can be any thing still more disgraceful, we have seen, for such an object, the utmost influence of the executive power, and every ministerial artifice, exerted without success. Nor can you ever succeed, unless *he* should be imprudent enough to forfeit the protection of those laws to which you owe your crown, or unless your ministers should persuade you to make it a question of force alone, and try the whole strength of government in opposition to the people. The lessons *he* has received from experience, will probably guard him from such excess of folly; and in your Majesty's virtues we find an unquestionable assurance that no illegal violence will be attempted.

Far from suspecting you of so horrible a design, we would attribute the continued violation of the laws, and even this last enormous attack upon the vital principles of the constitution, to an ill-advised, unworthy, personal resentment. From one false step you have been betrayed into another, and as the cause was unworthy of you, your ministers were determined that the prudence of the execution should correspond with the wisdom and dignity of the design. They have reduced you to the necessity of chusing out of a variety of difficulties;—to a situation so unhappy, that you can neither do wrong without ruin, nor right without affliction. These worthy servants have undoubtedly given you many singular proofs of their abilities. Not contented with making Mr Wilkes a man of importance, they have judiciously transferred the question, from the rights and interests of one man, to the most important rights and interests of the people, and forced your subjects, from wishing well to the cause of an individual, to unite with him in their own. Let them proceed as they have begun, and your Majesty need not doubt that the catastrophe will do no dishonour to the conduct of the piece.

The circumstances to which you are reduced, will not admit of a compromise with the English nation. Undecisive, qualifying measures will disgrace your government still more than open violence, and, without satisfying the people, will excite their contempt. They have too much understanding and spirit to accept of an indirect satisfaction for a direct injury. Nothing less than a repeal, as formal as the resolution itself, can heal the wound, which has been given to the constitution,[1] nor will any thing less be accepted. I can readily believe that there is an influence sufficient to recall that pernicious vote. The House of Commons undoubtedly consider their duty to the crown as paramount to all other obligations. To *us* they are only indebted for an accidental existence, and have justly transferred their gratitude from their parents to their benefactors;—from those who gave them birth, to the minister, from whose benevolence they derive the comforts and pleasures of their political life; — who has taken the tenderest care of their infancy, and relieves their necessities without offending their delicacy. But, if it were possible for their integrity to be degraded to a condition so vile and abject, that, compared with it, the present estimation they stand in is a state of honour and respect, consider, Sir, in what

---

[1] *I.e.* a repeal of the resolution excluding Wilkes from the House of Commons.

manner you will afterwards proceed. Can you conceive that the people of this country will long submit to be governed by so flexible a House of Commons! It is not in the nature of human society, that any form of government, in such circumstances, can long be preserved. In ours, the general contempt of the people is as fatal as their detestation. Such, I am persuaded, would be the necessary effect of any base concession made by the present House of Commons, and, as a qualifying measure would not be accepted, it remains for you to decide whether you will, at any hazard, support a set of men, who have reduced you to this unhappy dilemma, or whether you will gratify the united wishes of the whole people of England, by dissolving the parliament.

Taking it for granted, as I do very sincerely, that you have personally no design against the constitution, nor any views inconsistent with the good of your subjects, I think you cannot hesitate long upon the choice, which it equally concerns your interest and your honour to adopt. On one side, you hazard the affections of all your English subjects; you relinquish every hope of repose to yourself, and you endanger the establishment of your family for ever. All this you venture for no object whatsoever, or for such an object, as it would be an affront to you to name. Men of sense will examine your conduct with suspicion; while those who are incapable of comprehending to what degree they are injured, afflict you with clamours equally insolent and unmeaning. Supposing it possible that no fatal struggle should ensue, you determine at once to be unhappy, without the hope of a compensation either from interest or ambition. If an English king be hated or despised, he *must* be unhappy; and this perhaps is the only political truth, which he ought to be convinced of without experiment. But if the English people should no longer confine their resentment to a submissive representation of their wrongs; if, following the glorious example of their ancestors, they should no longer appeal to the creature of the constitution, but to that high Being, who gave them the rights of humanity, whose gifts it were sacrilege to surrender, let me ask you, Sir, upon what part of your subjects would you rely for assistance?

The people of Ireland have been uniformly plundered and oppressed. In return, they give you every day fresh marks of their resentment. They despise the miserable governor you have sent them,[1] because he is the creature of lord Bute; nor is it from any natural confusion in their ideas, that they are so ready to confound the original of a king with the disgraceful representation of him.

The distance of the colonies would make it impossible for them to take an active concern in your affairs, if they were as well affected to your government as they once pretended to be to your person. They were ready enough to distinguish between *you* and your ministers. They complained of an act of the legislature, but traced the origin of it no higher than to the servants of the crown: They pleased themselves with the hope that their sovereign, if not favourable to their cause, at least was impartial. The decisive, personal part you took against them, has effectually banished that first distinction from their minds. They consider you as united with your servants against America, and know how to distinguish the sovereign and a venal parliament on one side, from the real sentiments of the English people on the other. Looking forward to independence, they might possibly receive you for their king; but, if ever you

[1] George Townshend, fourth Viscount and first Marquis Townshend.

retire to America, be assured they will give you such a covenant to digest, as the presbytery of Scotland would have been ashamed to offer to Charles the Second. They left their native land in search of freedom, and found it in a desert. Divided as they are into a thousand forms of policy and religion, there is one point in which they all agree:—they equally detest the pageantry of a king, and the supercilious hypocrisy of a bishop.

It is not then from the alienated affections of Ireland or America, that you can reasonably look for assistance; still less from the people of England, who are actually contending for their rights, and in this great question, are parties against you. You are not, however, destitute of every appearance of support: You have all the Jacobites, Nonjurors, Roman Catholics, and Tories of this country, and all Scotland without exception.

Considering from what family you are descended, the choice of your friends has been singularly directed; and truly, Sir, if you had not lost the Whig interest of England, I should admire your dexterity in turning the hearts of your enemies. Is it possible for you to place any confidence in men, who, before they are faithful to you, must renounce every opinion, and betray every principle, both in church and state, which they inherit from their ancestors, and are confirmed in by their education? whose numbers are so inconsiderable, that they have long since been obliged to give up the principles and language which distinguish them as a party, and to fight under the banners of their enemies? Their zeal begins with hypocrisy, and must conclude in treachery. At first they deceive; at last they betray.

As to the Scotch, I must suppose your heart and understanding so biassed, from your earliest infancy, in their favour, that nothing less than *your own* misfortunes can undeceive you. You will not accept of the uniform experience of your ancestors: and when once a man is determined to believe, the very absurdity of the doctrine confirms him in his faith. A bigoted understanding can draw a proof of attachment to the house of Hanover from a notorious zeal for the house of Stuart, and find an earnest of future loyalty in former rebellions. Appearances are however in their favour: so strongly indeed, that one would think they had forgotten that you are their lawful king, and had mistaken you for a pretender to the crown. Let it be admitted then that the

Scotch are as sincere in their present professions, as if you were in reality not an Englishman, but a Briton of the North. You would not be the first prince, of their native country, against whom they have rebelled, nor the first whom they have basely betrayed. Have you forgotten, Sir, or has your favourite concealed from you, that part of our history, when the unhappy Charles (and he too had private virtues) fled from the open, avowed indignation of his English subjects, and surrendered himself at discretion to the good faith of his own countrymen. Without looking for support in their affections as subjects, he applied only to their honour as gentlemen, for protection. They received him as they would your Majesty, with bows and smiles, and falsehood, and kept him until they had settled their bargain with the English parliament; then basely sold their native king to the vengeance of his enemies. This, Sir, was not the act of a few traitors, but the deliberate treachery of a Scotch parliament, representing the nation. A wise prince might draw from it two lessons of equal utility to himself. On one side he might learn to dread the undisguised resentment of a generous people, who dare openly assert their rights, and who, in a just cause, are ready to meet their sovereign in the field. On the other side, he would be taught to apprehend something far more formidable;—a fawning treachery, against which no prudence can guard, no courage can defend. The insidious smile upon the cheek would warn him of the canker in the heart.

From the uses to which one part of the army has been too frequently applied, you have some reason to expect, that there are no services they would refuse. Here too we trace the partiality of your understanding. You take the sense of the army from the conduct of the guards, with the same justice with which you collect the sense of the people from the representations of the ministry. Your marching regiments, Sir, will not make the guards their example either as soldiers or subjects. They feel and resent, as they ought to do, that invariable, undistinguishing favour with which the guards are treated; while those gallant troops, by whom every hazardous, every laborious service is performed, are left to perish in garrisons abroad, or pine in quarters at home, neglected and forgotten. If they had no sense of the great original duty they owe their country, their resentment would operate like patriotism, and leave your cause to be defended by those to whom you have lavished the rewards and honours of their profession. The Prætorian bands, enervated and debauched as they were, had still strength enough to awe the Roman populace: but when the distant legions took the alarm, they marched to Rome, and gave away the empire.

On this side then, whichever way you turn your eyes, you see nothing but perplexity and distress. You may determine to support the very ministry who have reduced your affairs to this deplorable situation: you may shelter yourself under the forms of a parliament, and set your people at defiance. But be assured, Sir, that such a resolution would be as imprudent as it would be odious. If it did not immediately shake your establishment, it would rob you of your peace of mind for ever.

On the other, how different is the prospect! How easy, how safe and honourable is the path before you! The English nation declare they are grossly injured by their representatives, and solicit your Majesty to exert your lawful prerogative, and give them an opportunity of recalling a trust, which, they find, has been scandalously abused. You are not to be told that the power of the House of Commons is not original, but delegated to them for the welfare of the people, from whom they received it. A question of right arises between the constituent and the representative body. By what authority shall it be decided? Will your Majesty interfere in a question in which you have properly no immediate concern?—It would be a step equally odious and unnecessary. Shall the Lords be called upon to determine the rights and privileges of the Commons?— They cannot do it without a flagrant breach of the constitution. Or will you refer it to the judges?—They have often told your ancestors, that the law of parliament is above them. What party then remains, but to leave it to the people to determine for themselves? They alone are injured; and since there is no superior power, to which the cause can be referred, they alone ought to determine.

I do not mean to perplex you with a tedious argument upon a subject already so discussed that inspiration could hardly throw a new light upon it. There are, however, two points of view, in which it particularly imports your Majesty to consider the late proceedings of the House of Commons. By depriving a subject of his birthright, they have attributed to their own vote an authority equal to an act of the whole legislature; and, though perhaps not with the same motives, have strictly followed the example of the long parliament, which first declared the regal office useless, and soon after, with as little ceremony, dissolved the House of Lords. The same pretended power, which robs an English subject of his birthright, may rob an English king of his crown. In another view, the resolution of the House of Commons, apparently not so dangerous to your Majesty, is still more alarming to your people. Not contented with divesting one man of his right, they have arbitrarily conveyed that right to another. They have set aside a return as illegal, without daring to censure those officers, who were particularly apprized of Mr Wilkes's incapacity not only by the declaration of the House, but expressly by the writ directed to them, and who nevertheless returned him as duly elected. They have rejected the majority of votes, the only criterion by which our laws judge of the sense of the people; they have transferred the right of election from the collective to the representative body; and by these acts, taken separately or together, they have essentially altered the original constitution of the House of Commons. Versed, as your Majesty undoubtedly is, in the English history, it cannot easily escape you, how much it is your interest, as well as your duty, to prevent one of the three estates[1] from encroaching upon the province of the other two, or assuming the authority of them all. When once they have departed from the great constitutional line, by which all their proceedings should be directed, who will answer for their future moderation? Or what assurance will they give you, that, when they have trampled upon their equals, they will submit to a superior? Your Majesty may learn hereafter, how nearly the slave and tyrant are allied.

Some of your council, more candid than the rest, admit the abandoned profligacy of the present House of Commons, but oppose their dissolution upon an opinion, I confess not very unwarrantable, that their successors would be equally at the disposal of the Treasury. I cannot persuade myself that the nation will have profited so little by experience. But if that opinion were well founded,

---

[1] Junius here follows the popular error that the three estates were king, lords, and commons: the king is not an estate; and the three were properly the clergy, peers, and commons.

you might then gratify our wishes at an easy rate, and appease the present clamour against your government, without offering any material injury to the favourite cause of corruption.

You have still an honourable part to act. The affections of your subjects may still be recovered. But before you subdue *their* hearts, you must gain a noble victory over your own. Discard those little, personal resentments, which have too long directed your public conduct. Pardon this man the remainder of his punishment; and if resentment still prevails, make it, what it should have been long since, an act, not of mercy, but contempt. He will soon fall back into his natural station, —a silent senator, and hardly supporting the weekly eloquence of a newspaper. The gentle breath of peace would leave him on the surface, neglected and unremoved. It is only the tempest, that lifts him from his place.

Without consulting your minister, call together your whole council. Let it appear to the public that you can determine and act for yourself. Come forward to your people. Lay aside the wretched formalities of a king, and speak to your subjects with the spirit of a man, and in the language of a gentleman. Tell them you have been fatally deceived.

The acknowledgment will be no disgrace, but rather an honour to your understanding. Tell them you are determined to remove every cause of complaint against your government; that you will give your confidence to no man, who does not possess the confidence of your subjects; and leave it to themselves to determine, by their conduct at a future election, whether or no it be in reality the general sense of the nation, that their rights have been arbitrarily invaded by the present House of Commons, and the constitution betrayed. They will then do justice to their representatives and to themselves.

These sentiments, Sir, and the style they are conveyed in, may be offensive, perhaps, because they are new to you. Accustomed to the language of courtiers, you measure their affections by the vehemence of their expressions; and, when they only praise you indirectly, you admire their sincerity. But this is not a time to trifle with your fortune. They deceive you, Sir, who tell you that you have many friends, whose affections are founded upon a principle of personal attachment. The first foundation of friendship is not the power of conferring benefits, but the equality with which they are received, and *may* be returned. The fortune, which made you a king, forbade you to have a friend. It is a law of nature which cannot be violated with impunity. The mistaken prince, who looks for friendship, will find a favourite, and in that favourite the ruin of his affairs.

The people of England are loyal to the house of Hanover, not from a vain preference of one family to another, but from a conviction that the establishment of that family was necessary to the support of their civil and religious liberties. This, Sir, is a principle of allegiance equally solid and rational;—fit for Englishmen to adopt, and well worthy of your Majesty's encouragement. We cannot long be deluded by nominal distinctions. The name of Stuart, of itself, is only contemptible; —armed with the sovereign authority, their principles are formidable. The prince who imitates their conduct, should be warned by their example; and while he plumes himself upon the security of his title to the crown, should remember that, as it was acquired by one revolution, it may be lost by another.

XII

THOUGHTS ON THE CAUSE OF THE PRESENT DISCONTENTS

[Burke appears to have commenced this pamphlet in May 1769, and it was published in 1770. He was therefore writing it at the same time that Junius was sending his letters to the proprietor of the *Public Advertiser*, and both writers deal with the same political conditions, but in a very different manner. Junius writes merely as a brilliant partisan, Burke as a statesman. This is the earliest of his great writings, but the fragment reprinted here probably contains more sound political philosophy than is to be found anywhere else in the same space.][1]

Hoc vero occultum, intestinum ac domesticum malum, non modo non existit, verum etiam opprimit, antequam prospicere atque explorare potueris.—CICERO.[2]

IT is an undertaking of some degree of delicacy to examine into the cause of public disorders. If a man happens not to succeed in such an enquiry, he will be thought weak and visionary;

---

[1] See Introd. 21.
[2] In Verrem. Oratio Secunda, I. xv., § 39.

if he touches the true grievance, there is a danger that he may come near to persons of weight and consequence, who will rather be exasperated at the discovery of their errors, than thankful for the occasion of correcting them. If he should be obliged to blame the favourites of the people, he will be considered as the tool of power; if he censures those in power, he will be looked on as an instrument of faction. But in all exertions of duty something is to be hazarded. In cases of tumult and disorder, our law has invested every man, in some sort, with the authority of a magistrate. When the affairs of the nation are distracted, private people are, by the spirit of that law, justified in stepping a little out of their ordinary sphere. They enjoy a privilege, of somewhat more dignity and effect, than that of idle lamentation over the calamities of their country. They may look into them narrowly; they may reason upon them liberally; and if they should be so fortunate as to discover the true source of the mischief, and to suggest any probable method of removing it, though they may displease the rulers for the day, they are certainly of service to the cause of Government. Government is deeply interested in everything which, even through the medium of some temporary uneasiness, may tend finally to compose the minds of the subject, and to conciliate their affections. I have nothing to do here with the abstract value of the voice of the people. But as long as reputation, the most precious possession of every individual, and as long as opinion, the great support of the State, depend entirely upon that voice, it can never be considered as a thing of little consequence either to individuals or to Government. Nations are not primarily ruled by laws; less by violence. Whatever original energy may be supposed either in force or regulation; the operation of both is, in truth, merely instrumental. Nations are governed by the same methods, and on the same principles, by which an individual without authority is often able to govern those who are his equals or his superiors; by a knowledge of their temper, and by a judicious management of it; I mean, —when public affairs are steadily and quietly conducted: not when Government is nothing but a continued scuffle between the magistrate and the multitude; in which sometimes the one and sometimes the other is uppermost; in which they alternately yield and prevail, in a series of contemptible victories, and scandalous submissions. The temper of the people amongst whom he presides ought therefore to be the first study of a Statesman. And the knowledge of this temper it is by no means impossible for him to attain, if he has not an interest in being ignorant of what it is his duty to learn.

To complain of the age we live in, to murmur at the present possessors of power, to lament the past, to conceive extravagant hopes of the future, are the common dispositions of the greatest part of mankind; indeed the necessary effects of the ignorance and levity of the vulgar. Such complaints and humours have existed in all times; yet as all times have *not* been alike, true political sagacity manifests itself, in distinguishing that complaint which only characterizes the general infirmity of human nature, from those which are symptoms of the particular distemperature of our own air and season.

NOBODY, I believe, will consider it merely as the language of spleen or disappointment, if I say, that there is something particularly alarming in the present conjuncture. There is hardly a man, in or out of power, who holds any other language. That Government is at once dreaded and contemned; that the laws are despoiled of all their respected and salutary terrors; that their inaction is a subject of ridicule, and their exertion of abhorrence; that rank, and office, and title, and all the solemn plausibilities of the world, have lost their reverence and effect; that our foreign politicks are as much deranged as our domestic œconomy; that our dependencies are slackened in their affection, and loosened from their obedience; that we know neither how to yield nor how to enforce; that hardly anything above or below, abroad or at home, is sound and entire; but that disconnection and confusion, in offices, in parties, in families, in Parliament, in the nation, prevail beyond the disorders of any former time: these are facts universally admitted and lamented.

This state of things is the more extraordinary, because the great parties which formerly divided and agitated the kingdom are known to be in a manner entirely dissolved.[1] No great external calamity has

---

[1] The Whig party had split up into a number of factions; the old Tory party of Queen Anne's time had been wiped out; Bolingbroke had called for a national party and a patriot king who should govern by the ablest men irrespective of party. Chatham had attempted a similar policy. Hence the results that Burke describes.

visited the nation; no pestilence or famine. We do not labour at present under any scheme of taxation new or oppressive in the quantity or in the mode. Nor are we engaged in unsuccessful war; in which, our misfortunes might easily pervert our judgment; and our minds, sore from the loss of national glory, might feel every blow of Fortune as a crime in Government.

It is impossible that the cause of this strange distemper should not sometimes become a subject of discourse. It is a compliment due, and which I willingly pay, to those who administer our affairs, to take notice in the first place of their speculation. Our Ministers are of opinion, that the increase of our trade and manufactures, that our growth by colonization and by conquest, have concurred to accumulate immense wealth in the hands of some individuals; and this again being dispersed amongst the people, has rendered them universally proud, ferocious, and ungovernable; that the insolence of some from their enormous wealth, and the boldness of others from a guilty poverty, have rendered them capable of the most atrocious attempts; so that they have trampled upon all subordination, and violently borne down the unarmed laws of a free Government; barriers too feeble against the fury of a populace so fierce and licentious as ours. They contend, that no adequate provocation has been given for so spreading a discontent; our affairs having been conducted throughout with remarkable temper and consummate wisdom. The wicked industry of some libellers,[1] joined to the intrigues of a few disappointed politicians, have, in their opinion, been able to produce this unnatural ferment in the nation.

Nothing indeed can be more unnatural than the present convulsions of this country, if the above account be a true one. I confess I shall assent to it with great reluctance, and only on the compulsion of the clearest and firmest proofs; because their account resolves itself into this short, but discouraging proposition, 'That we have a very good Ministry, but that we are a very bad people;' that we set ourselves to bite the hand that feeds us; that with a malignant insanity we oppose the measures, and ungratefully vilify the persons, of those whose sole object is our own peace and prosperity. If a few puny libellers, acting under a knot of factious

[1] Especially Junius.

politicians, without virtue, parts, or character, (such they are constantly represented by these gentlemen,) are sufficient to excite this disturbance, very perverse must be the disposition of that people, amongst whom such a disturbance can be excited by such means. It is besides no small aggravation of the public misfortune, that the disease, on this hypothesis, appears to be without remedy. If the wealth of the nation be the cause of its turbulence, I imagine it is not proposed to introduce poverty, as a constable to keep the peace. If our dominions abroad are the roots which feed all this rank luxuriance of sedition, it is not intended to cut them off in order to famish the fruit. If our liberty has enfeebled the executive power, there is no design, I hope, to call in the aid of despotism, to fill up the deficiencies of law. Whatever may be intended, these things are not yet professed. We seem therefore to be driven to absolute despair; for we have no other materials to work upon, but those out of which God has been pleased to form the inhabitants of this island. If these be radically and essentially vitious, all that can be said is that those men are very unhappy, to whose fortune or duty it falls to administer the affairs of this untoward people. I hear it indeed sometimes asserted, that a steady perseverance in the present measures, and a rigorous punishment of those who oppose them, will in course of time infallibly put an end to these disorders. But this, in my opinion, is said without much observation of our present disposition, and without any knowledge at all of the general nature of mankind. If the matter of which this nation is composed be so very fermentable as these gentlemen describe it, leaven never will be wanting to work it up, as long as discontent, revenge, and ambition have existence in the world. Particular punishments are the cure for accidental distempers in the State; they inflame rather than allay those heats which arise from the settled mismanagement of the Government, or from a natural ill disposition in the people. It is of the utmost moment not to make mistakes in the use of strong measures; and firmness is then only a virtue when it accompanies the most perfect wisdom. In truth, inconstancy is a sort of natural corrective of folly and ignorance.

I am not one of those who think that the people are never in the wrong. They have been so, frequently and outrageously, both in other countries and in this. But I do say, that in all disputes between them and their rulers, the presumption is at least upon a par in favour of the people. Experience may perhaps justify me in going further. When popular discontents have been very prevalent; it may well be affirmed and supported, that there has been generally something found amiss in the constitution, or in the conduct of Government. The people have no interest in disorder. When they do wrong, it is their error, and not their crime. But with the governing part of the State, it is far otherwise. They certainly may act ill by design, as well as by mistake. '*Les révolutions qui arrivent dans les grands états ne sont point un effect du hazard, ni du caprice des peuples. Rien ne révolte* les grands *d'un royaume comme* un Gouvernement foible et dérangé. *Pour la* populace, *ce n'est jamais par envie d'attaquer qu'elle se soulève, mais par impatience de souffrir.*'[1] These are the words of a great man; of a Minister of state; and a zealous assertor of Monarchy. They are applied to the *system of Favouritism* which was adopted by Henry the Third of France, and to the dreadful consequences it produced. What he says of revolutions, is equally true of all great disturbances. If this presumption in favour of the subjects against the trustees

---

[1] Sully's Memoirs, i. 133; Sully was minister to Henry IV. of France.

of power be not the more probable, I am sure it is the more comfortable speculation; because it is more easy to change an administration than to reform a people.

Upon a supposition, therefore, that, in the opening of the cause, the presumptions stand equally balanced between the parties, there seems sufficient ground to entitle any person to a fair hearing, who attempts some other scheme beside that easy one which is fashionable in some fashionable companies, to account for the present discontents. It is not to be argued that we endure no grievance, because our grievances are not of the same sort with those under which we laboured formerly; not precisely those which we bore from the Tudors, or vindicated on the Stuarts. A great change has taken place in the affairs of this country. For in the silent lapse of events as material alterations have been insensibly brought about in the policy and character of governments and nations, as those which have been marked by the tumult of public revolutions.

It is very rare indeed for men to be wrong in their feelings concerning public misconduct; as rare to be right in their speculation upon

the cause of it. I have constantly observed,
that the generality of people are fifty years,
at least, behindhand in their politicks. There
are but very few, who are capable of comparing and digesting what passes before their
eyes at different times and occasions, so as
to form the whole into a distinct system. But
in books everything is settled for them, without the exertion of any considerable diligence
or sagacity. For which reason men are wise
with but little reflexion, and good with little
self-denial, in the business of all times except
their own. We are very uncorrupt and tolerably enlightened judges of the transactions of
past ages; where no passions deceive, and
where the whole train of circumstances, from
the trifling cause to the tragical event, is set
in an orderly series before us. Few are the
partizans of departed tyranny; and to be a
Whig on the business of an hundred years
ago, is very consistent with every advantage
of present servility. This retrospective wisdom,
and historical patriotism, are things of wonderful convenience; and serve admirably to reconcile the old quarrel between speculation
and practice. Many a stern republican, after
gorging himself with a full feast of admiration of the Grecian commonwealths and of

our true Saxon constitution, and discharging all the splendid bile of his virtuous indignation on King John and King James, sits down perfectly satisfied to the coarsest work and homeliest job of the day he lives in. I believe there was no professed admirer of Henry the Eighth among the instruments of the last King James; nor in the court of Henry the Eighth was there, I dare say, to be found a single advocate for the favourites of Richard the Second.

No complaisance to our Court, or to our age, can make me believe nature to be so changed, but that public liberty will be among us, as among our ancestors, obnoxious to some person or other; and that opportunities will be furnished for attempting, at least, some alteration to the prejudice of our constitution. These attempts will naturally vary in their mode, according to times and circumstances. For ambition, though it has ever the same general views, has not at all times the same means, nor the same particular objects. A great deal of the furniture of ancient tyranny is worn to rags; the rest is entirely out of fashion. Besides, there are few Statesmen so very clumsy and awkward in their business, as to fall into the identical snare which has proved fatal to their predecessors. When an arbitrary imposition is attempted upon the subject, undoubtedly it will not bear on its forehead the name of *Ship-money*. There is no danger that an extension of the *Forest laws* should be the chosen mode of oppression in this age. . . .

Every age has its own manners, and its politicks dependent upon them; and the same attempts will not be made against a constitution fully formed and matured, that were used to destroy it in the cradle, or to resist its growth during its infancy.

Against the being of Parliament, I am satisfied, no designs have ever been entertained since the Revolution. Every one must perceive, that it is strongly the interest of the Court, to have some second cause interposed between the Ministers and the people. The gentlemen of the House of Commons have an interest equally strong, in sustaining the part of that intermediate cause. However they may hire out the *usufruct* of their voices, they never will part with the *fee and inheritance*. Accordingly those who have been of the most known devotion to the will and pleasure of a Court, have, at the same time, been most forward in asserting an high authority in the House of Commons. When they knew who were to use that authority, and how it was to be employed, they thought it never could be carried too far. It must be always the wish of an unconstitutional Statesman, that an House of Commons who are entirely dependent upon him, should have every right of the people entirely dependent upon their pleasure. It was soon discovered, that the forms of a free, and the ends of an arbitrary Government, were things not altogether incompatible.

The power of the Crown, almost dead and rotten as Prerogative, has grown up anew, with much more strength, and far less odium, under the name of Influence. An influence, which operated without noise and without violence; an influence, which converted the very antagonist, into the instrument, of power; which contained in itself a perpetual principle of growth and renovation; and which the distresses and the prosperity of the country equally tended to augment, was an admirable substitute for a Prerogative, that, being only the offspring of antiquated prejudices, had moulded in its original stamina irresistible principles of decay and dissolution. The ignorance of the people is a bottom but for a temporary system; the interest of active men in the State is a foundation perpetual and infallible. However, some circumstances, arising, it must be confessed, in a great degree from accident, prevented the effects of this influence for a long time from breaking out in a manner capable of exciting any serious apprehensions. Although Government was strong and flourished exceedingly, the *Court* had drawn far less advantage than one would imagine from this great source of power.

AT the Revolution, the Crown, deprived, for the ends of the Revolution itself, of many prerogatives, was found too weak to struggle against all the difficulties which pressed so new and unsettled a Government. The Court was obliged therefore to delegate a part of its powers to men of such interest as could support, and of such fidelity as would adhere to, its establishment. Such men were able to draw in a greater number to a concurrence in the common defence. This connexion, necessary at first, continued long after convenient; and properly conducted might indeed, in all situations, be an useful instrument of Government. At the same time, through the intervention of men of popular weight and character, the people possessed a security for their just proportion of importance in the State. But as the title to the Crown grew stronger by long possession, and by the constant increase of its influence, these helps have of late seemed to certain persons no better than incumbrances. The powerful managers for Government were not sufficiently submissive to the pleasure of the possessors of immediate and personal favour, sometimes from a confidence in their own strength natural and acquired; sometimes from a fear of offending their friends, and weakening that lead in the country, which gave them a consideration independent of the Court. Men acted as if the Court could receive, as well as confer, an obligation. The influence of Government, thus divided in appearance between the Court and the leaders of parties, became in many cases an accession rather to the popular than to the royal scale; and some part of that influence, which would otherwise have been possessed as in a sort of mortmain and unalienable domain, returned again to the great ocean from whence it arose, and circulated among the people. This method therefore of governing by men of great natural interest or great acquired consideration, was viewed in a very invidious light by the true lovers of absolute monarchy. It is the nature of despotism to abhor power held by any means but its own momentary pleasure; and to annihilate all intermediate situations between boundless strength on its own part, and total debility on the part of the people.

To get rid of all this intermediate and independent importance, and *to secure to the Court the unlimited and uncontrouled use of its own vast influence, under the sole direction of its own private favour*, has for some years past been the great object of policy. If this were compassed, the influence of the Crown must of course produce all the effects which the most sanguine partizans of the Court could possibly desire. Government might then be carried on without any concurrence on the part of the people; without any attention to the dignity of the greater, or to the affections of the lower sorts. A new project was therefore devised by a certain set of intriguing men, totally different from the system of Administration which had prevailed since the accession of the House of Brunswick. This project, I have heard, was first conceived by some persons in the court of Frederick Prince of Wales.

The earliest attempt in the execution of this design was to set up for Minister, a person, in rank indeed respectable, and very ample in fortune; but who, to the moment of this vast and sudden elevation, was little known or considered in the kingdom.[1] To him the whole

---

[1] Bute; the design was originated by Bolingbroke in his 'Patriot King.' Bute became virtual prime minister

nation was to yield an immediate and implicit submission. But whether it was from want of firmness to bear up against the first opposition; or that things were not yet fully ripened, or that this method was not found the most eligible; that idea was soon abandoned. The instrumental part of the project was a little altered, to accommodate it to the time, and to bring things more gradually and more surely to the one great end proposed.

The first part of the reformed plan was to draw *a line which should separate the Court from the Ministry.* Hitherto these names had been looked upon as synonymous; but for the future, Court and Administration were to be considered as things totally distinct. By this operation, two systems of Administration were to be formed; one which should be in the real secret and confidence; the other merely ostensible, to perform the official and executory duties of Government. The latter were alone to be responsible; whilst the real advisers, who enjoyed all the power, were effectually removed from all the danger.[1]

on the resignation of Pitt in October 1761, but his tenure of office only lasted till April 1763.

[1] Curiously enough, there was a somewhat similar double system in France under Louis XV. His osten-

Secondly, *A party under these leaders was to be formed in favour of the Court against the Ministry:* this party was to have a large share in the emoluments of Government, and to hold it totally separate from, and independent of, ostensible Administration.

The third point, and that on which the success of the whole scheme ultimately depended, was *to bring Parliament to an acquiescence in this project.* Parliament was therefore to be taught by degrees a total indifference to the persons, rank, influence, abilities, connexions, and character of the Ministers of the Crown. By means of a discipline, on which I shall say more hereafter, that body was to be habituated to the most opposite interests, and the most discordant politicks. All connexions and dependencies among subjects were to be entirely dissolved. As hitherto business had gone through the hands of leaders of Whigs or Tories, men of talents to conciliate the people, and to engage their confidence, now the method was to be altered; and the lead was to be given to men of no sort of consideration or credit in the country. This want of natural importance was to be their very title to dele-

---

sible ministers were continually thwarted by secret agents who were in the full confidence of the king.

gated power. Members of Parliament were to be hardened into an insensibility to pride as well as to duty. Those high and haughty sentiments, which are the great support of independence, were to be let down gradually. Point of honour and precedence were no more to be regarded in Parliamentary decorum, than in a Turkish army. It was to be avowed, as a constitutional maxim, that the King might appoint one of his footmen, or one of your footmen, for Minister; and that he ought to be, and that he would be, as well followed as the first name for rank or wisdom in the nation. Thus Parliament was to look on, as if perfectly unconcerned, while a cabal of the closet and back-stairs was substituted in the place of a national Administration.

With such a degree of acquiescence, any measure of any Court might well be deemed thoroughly secure. The capital objects, and by much the most flattering characteristicks of arbitrary power, would be obtained. Everything would be drawn from its holdings in the country to the personal favour and inclination of the Prince. This favour would be the sole introduction to power, and the only tenure by which it was to be held: so that no person looking towards another, and all looking towards the Court, it was impossible but that the motive which solely influenced every man's hopes must come in time to govern every man's conduct; till at last the servility became universal, in spite of the dead letter of any laws or institutions whatsoever.

How it should happen that any man could be tempted to venture upon such a project of Government, may at first view appear surprizing. But the fact is, that opportunities very inviting to such an attempt have offered; and the scheme itself was not destitute of some arguments, not wholly unplausible, to recommend it. These opportunities and these arguments, the use that has been made of both, the plan for carrying this new scheme of government into execution, and the effects which it has produced, are in my opinion worthy of our serious consideration.

His Majesty came to the throne of these kingdoms with more advantages than any of his predecessors since the Revolution. Fourth in descent, and third in succession of his Royal family, even the zealots of hereditary right, in him, saw something to flatter their favourite prejudices; and to justify a transfer of their attachments, without a change in their principles. The person and cause of the Pretender were become contemptible; his title disowned throughout Europe, his party disbanded in England. His Majesty came indeed to the inheritance of a mighty war; but, victorious in every part of the globe, peace was always in his power, not to negociate, but to dictate. No foreign habitudes or attachments withdrew him from the cultivation of his power at home. His revenue for the civil establishment, fixed (as it was then thought) at a large, but definite sum,[1] was ample, without being invidious. His influence, by additions from conquest, by an augmentation of debt, by an increase of military and naval establishment, much strengthened and extended. And coming to the throne in the prime and full vigour of youth, as from affection there was a strong dislike, so from dread there seemed to be a general averseness, from giving anything like offence to a Monarch, against whose resentment opposition could not look for a refuge in any sort of reversionary hope.

These singular advantages inspired his Majesty only with a more ardent desire to preserve unimpaired the spirit of that national freedom, to which he owed a situa-

[1] £800,000.

tion so full of glory. But to others it suggested sentiments of a very different nature. They thought they now beheld an opportunity (by a certain sort of Statesmen never long undiscovered or unemployed) of drawing to themselves, by the aggrandisement of a Court Faction, a degree of power which they could never hope to derive from natural influence or from honourable service; and which it was impossible they could hold with the least security, whilst the system of Administration rested upon its former bottom. In order to facilitate the execution of their design, it was necessary to make many alterations in political arrangement, and a signal change in the opinions, habits, and connexions of the greatest part of those who at that time acted in publick.

In the first place, they proceeded gradually, but not slowly, to destroy everything of strength which did not derive its principal nourishment from the immediate pleasure of the Court. The greatest weight of popular opinion and party connexion were then with the Duke of Newcastle and Mr Pitt. Neither of these held their importance by the *new tenure* of the Court; they were not therefore thought to be so proper as others for the services which were required by that tenure. It happened very favourably for the new system, that under a forced coalition there rankled an incurable alienation and disgust between the parties which composed the Administration. Mr Pitt was first attacked. Not satisfied with removing him from power, they endeavoured by various artifices to ruin his character. The other party seemed rather pleased to get rid of so oppressive a support; not perceiving that their own fall was prepared by his, and involved in it. Many other reasons prevented them from daring to look their true situation in the face. To the great Whig families it was extremely disagreeable, and seemed almost unnatural, to oppose the Administration of a Prince of the House of Brunswick. Day after day they hesitated, and doubted, and lingered, expecting that other counsels would take place; and were slow to be persuaded, that all which had been done by the Cabal, was the effect not of humour, but of system. It was more strongly and evidently the interest of the new Court Faction, to get rid of the great Whig connexions, than to destroy Mr Pitt. The power of that gentleman was vast indeed and merited; but it was in a great degree personal, and therefore transient. Theirs was rooted in the country. For, with a good deal less of popularity, they possessed a far more natural and fixed influence. Long possession of Government; vast property; obligations of favours given and received; connexion of office; ties of blood, of alliance, of friendship (things at that time supposed of some force); the name of Whig, dear to the majority of the people; the zeal early begun and steadily continued to the Royal Family: all these together formed a body of power in the nation, which was criminal and devoted. The great ruling principle of the Cabal, and that which animated and harmonized all their proceedings, how various soever they may have been, was to signify to the world, that the Court would proceed upon its own proper forces only; and that the pretence of bringing any other into its service was an affront to it, and not a support. Therefore when the chiefs were removed, in order to go to the root, the whole party was put under a proscription, so general and severe as to take their hard-earned bread from the lowest officers, in a manner which had never been known before, even in general revolutions. But it was thought necessary effectually to destroy all dependencies but one; and to show an example of the firmness and rigour with which the new system was to be supported.

Thus for the time were pulled down, in the persons of the Whig leaders and of Mr Pitt, (in spite of the services of the one at the accession of the Royal Family, and the recent services of the other in the war,) the *two only securities for the importance of the people; power arising from popularity; and power arising from connexion.* Here and there indeed a few individuals were left standing, who gave security for their total estrangement from the odious principles of party connexion and personal attachment; and it must be confessed that most of them have religiously kept their faith. Such a change could not however be made without a mighty shock to Government.

To reconcile the minds of the people to all these movements, principles correspondent to them had been preached up with great zeal. Every one must remember that the Cabal set out with the most astonishing prudery, both moral and political. Those, who in a few months after soused over head and ears into the deepest and dirtiest pits of corruption, cried out violently against the indirect practices in the electing and managing of Parliaments, which had formerly prevailed. This marvellous abhorrence which the Court had suddenly taken to all influence, was not only circulated in conversation through the kingdom, but pompously announced to the publick, with many other extraordinary things, in a pamphlet[1] which had all the appearance of a manifesto preparatory to some considerable enterprize. Throughout, it was a satire, though in terms managed and decent enough, on the politicks of the former Reign. It was indeed written with no small art and address.

In this piece appeared the first dawning of the new system; there first appeared the idea (then only in speculation) of *separating the Court from the Administration;* of carrying everything from national connexion to personal regards; and of forming a regular party for that purpose, under the name of *King's men.*

To recommend this system to the people, a perspective view of the Court, gorgeously painted, and finely illuminated from within, was exhibited to the gaping multitude. Party was to be totally done away, with all its evil

[1] Lord Bath's 'Seasonable Hints from an Honest Man, 1761. William Pulteney, Earl of Bath, was long a political ally of Bolingbroke, and imbibed his ideas about a 'Patriot King.'

works. Corruption was to be cast down from Court, as *Atè* was from heaven. Power was thenceforward to be the chosen residence of public spirit; and no one was to be supposed under any sinister influence, except those who had the misfortune to be in disgrace at Court, which was to stand in lieu of all vices and all corruptions. A scheme of perfection to be realized in a Monarchy, far beyond the visionary Republick of Plato. The whole scenery was exactly disposed to captivate those good souls, whose credulous morality is so invaluable a treasure to crafty politicians. Indeed there was wherewithall to charm every body, except those few who are not much pleased with professions of supernatural virtue, who know of what stuff such professions are made, for what purposes they are designed, and in what they are sure constantly to end. Many innocent gentlemen, who had been talking prose all their lives without knowing anything of the matter, began at last to open their eyes upon their own merits, and to attribute their not having been Lords of the Treasury and Lords of Trade many years before, merely to the prevalence of party, and to the Ministerial power, which had frustrated the good intentions of the Court in favour of their abilities. Now was the time to unlock the sealed fountain of Royal bounty, which had been infamously monopolized and huckstered, and to let it flow at large upon the whole people. The time was come, to restore Royalty to its original splendour. *Mettre le Roy hors de page*, became a sort of watchword. And it was constantly in the mouths of all the runners of the Court, that nothing could preserve the balance of the constitution from being overturned by the rabble, or by a faction of the nobility, but to free the sovereign effectually from that Ministerial tyranny under which the Royal dignity had been oppressed in the person of his Majesty's grandfather.

These were some of the many artifices used to reconcile the people to the great change which was made in the persons who composed the Ministry, and the still greater which was made and avowed in its constitution. As to individuals, other methods were employed with them; in order so thoroughly to disunite every party, and even every family, that *no concert, order, or effect, might appear in any future opposition.* And in this manner an Administration without connexion with the people, or with one another, was first put in possession of Government. What good consequences followed from it, we have all seen; whether with regard to virtue, public or private; to the case and happiness of the Sovereign; or to the real strength of Government. But as so much stress was then laid on the necessity of this new project, it will not be amiss to take a view of the effects of this Royal servitude and vile durance, which was so deplored in the reign of the late Monarch, and was so carefully to be avoided in the reign of his Successor. The effects were these.

In times full of doubt and danger to his person and family, George the Second maintained the dignity of his Crown connected with the liberty of his people, not only unimpaired, but improved, for the space of thirty-three years. He overcame a dangerous rebellion, abetted by foreign force, and raging in the heart of his kingdoms; and thereby destroyed the seeds of all future rebellion that could arise upon the same principle. He carried the glory, the power, the commerce of England, to an height unknown even to this renowned nation in the times of its greatest prosperity: and he left his succession resting on the true and only true foundation of all national and all regal greatness; affection at home, reputation abroad, trust in allies, terror in rival nations. The most ardent lover of his country cannot wish for Great Britain an happier fate than to continue as she was then left. A people emulous as we are in affection to our present Sovereign, know not how to form a prayer to Heaven for a greater blessing upon his virtues, or an higher state of felicity and glory, than that he should live, and should reign, and, when Providence ordains it, should die, exactly like his illustrious Predecessor.

A great Prince may be obliged (though such a thing cannot happen very often) to sacrifice his private inclination to his public interest. A wise Prince will not think that such a restraint implies a condition of servility; and truly, if such was the condition of the last reign, and the effects were also such as we have described, we ought, no less for the sake of the Sovereign whom we love, than for our own, to hear arguments convincing indeed, before we depart from the maxims of that reign, or fly in the face of this great body of strong and recent experience.

One of the principal topicks which was then, and has been since, much employed by that political school, is an effectual terror of the growth of an aristocratic power, prejudicial to the rights of the Crown, and the balance of the constitution. Any new powers exercised in the House of Lords, or in the House of Commons, or by the Crown, ought certainly to excite the vigilant and anxious jealousy of a free people. Even a new and unprecedented course of action in the whole Legislature, without great and evident reason, may be a subject of just uneasiness. I will not affirm, that there may not have lately appeared in the House of Lords a disposition to some attempts derogatory to the legal rights of the subject. If any such have really appeared, they have arisen, not from a power properly aristocratic, but from the same influence which is charged with having excited attempts of a similar nature in the House of Commons; which House, if it should have been betrayed into an unfortunate quarrel with its constituents, and involved in a charge of the very same nature, could have neither power nor inclination to repel such attempts in others. Those attempts in the House of Lords can no more be called aristocratic proceedings, than the proceedings with regard to the county of Middlesex[1] in the House of Commons can with any sense be called democratical.

It is true, that the Peers have a great influence in the kingdom, and in every part of the

---

[1] *I.e.* in connection with Wilkes's election.

public concerns. While they are men of property, it is impossible to prevent it, except by such means as must prevent all property from its natural operation: an event not easily to be compassed, while property is power; nor by any means to be wished, while the least notion exists of the method by which the spirit of liberty acts, and of the means by which it is preserved. If any particular Peers, by their uniform, upright, constitutional conduct, by their public and their private virtues, have acquired an influence in the country; the people on whose favour that influence depends, and from whom it arose, will never be duped into an opinion, that such greatness in a Peer is the despotism of an aristocracy, when they know and feel it to be the effect and pledge of their own importance.

I am no friend to aristocracy, in the sense at least in which that word is usually understood. If it were not a bad habit to moot cases on the supposed ruin of the constitution, I should be free to declare, that if it must perish, I would rather by far see it resolved into any other form, than lost in that austere and insolent domination. But, whatever my dislikes may be, my fears are not upon that quarter. The question, on the influence of a Court, and of a

Peerage, is not, which of the two dangers is the most eligible, but which is the most imminent. He is but a poor observer, who has not seen, that the generality of Peers, far from supporting themselves in a state of independent greatness, are but too apt to fall into an oblivion of their proper dignity, and to run headlong into an abject servitude. Would to God it were true, that the fault of our Peers were too much spirit! It is worthy of some observation, that these gentlemen, so jealous of aristocracy, make no complaints of the power of those peers (neither few nor inconsiderable) who are always in the train of a Court, and whose whole weight must be considered as a portion of the settled influence of the Crown. This is all safe and right; but if some Peers (I am very sorry they are not as many as they ought to be) set themselves, in the great concern of Peers and Commons, against a back-stairs influence and clandestine government, then the alarm begins; then the constitution is in danger of being forced into an aristocracy.

I rest a little the longer on this Court topick, because it was much insisted upon at the time of the great change, and has been since frequently revived by many of the agents of that party: for, whilst they are terrifying the great and opulent with the horrors of mob-government, they are by other managers attempting (though hitherto with little success) to alarm the people with a phantom of tyranny in the Nobles. All this is done upon their favourite principle of disunion, of sowing jealousies amongst the different orders of the State, and of disjointing the natural strength of the kingdom; that it may be rendered incapable of resisting the sinister designs of wicked men, who have engrossed the Royal power.

THUS much of the topicks chosen by the Courtiers to recommend their system; it will be necessary to open a little more at large the nature of that party which was formed for its support. Without this, the whole would have been no better than a visionary amusement, like the scheme of Harrington's political club,[1] and not a business in which the nation had a real concern. As a powerful party, and a party constructed on a new principle, it is a very inviting object of curiosity.

---

[1] James Harrington (1611-1677), the author of 'Oceana,' during the confusion that followed Cromwell's death, formed a club called the 'Rota' to discuss the introduction of his political schemes. It lasted from Nov. 1659 to Feb. 1660, when Monck's action made the Restoration a certainty. *Cf.* Hudibras, Part II., Canto iii. 1107.

It must be remembered, that since the Revolution, until the period we are speaking of, the influence of the Crown had been always employed in supporting the Ministers of State, and in carrying on the public business according to their opinions. But the party now in question is formed upon a very different idea. It is to intercept the favour, protection, and confidence of the Crown in the passage to its Ministers; it is to come between them and their importance in Parliament; it is to separate them from all their natural and acquired dependencies; it is intended as the controul, not the support, of Administration. The machinery of this system is perplexed in its movements, and false in its principle. It is formed on a supposition that the King is something external to his government; and that he may be honoured and aggrandized, even by its debility and disgrace. The plan proceeds expressly on the idea of enfeebling the regular executory power. It proceeds on the idea of weakening the State in order to strengthen the Court. The scheme depending entirely on distrust, on disconnexion, on mutability by principle, on systematic weakness in every particular member; it is impossible that the total result should be substantial strength of any kind.

As a foundation of their scheme, the Cabal have established a sort of *Rota* in the Court. All sorts of parties, by this means, have been brought into Administration, from whence few have had the good fortune to escape without disgrace; none at all without considerable losses. In the beginning of each arrangement no professions of confidence and support are wanting, to induce the leading men to engage. But while the Ministers of the day appear in all the pomp and pride of power, while they have all their canvas spread out to the wind, and every sail filled with the fair and prosperous gale of Royal favour, in a short time they find, they know not how, a current, which sets directly against them; which prevents all progress; and even drives them backwards. They grow ashamed and mortified in a situation, which, by its vicinity to power, only serves to remind them the more strongly of their insignificance. They are obliged either to execute the orders of their inferiors, or to see themselves opposed by the natural instruments of their office. With the loss of their dignity, they lose their temper. In their turn they grow troublesome to that Cabal, which, whether it supports or opposes, equally disgraces and equally betrays them. It is soon found necessary to get rid of the heads of Administration; but it is of the heads only. As there always are many rotten members belonging to the best connexions, it is not hard to persuade several to continue in office without their leaders. By this means the party goes out much thinner than it came in; and is only reduced in strength by its temporary possession of power. Besides, if by accident, or in course of changes, that power should be recovered, the Junto have thrown up a retrenchment of these carcases, which may serve to cover themselves in a day of danger. They conclude, not unwisely, that such rotten members will become the first objects of disgust and resentment to their antient connexions.

They contrive to form in the outward Administration two parties at the least; which, whilst they are tearing one another to pieces, are both competitors for the favour and protection of the Cabal; and, by their emulation, contribute to throw everything more and more into the hands of the interior managers.

A Minister of State will sometimes keep himself totally estranged from all his colleagues; will differ from them in their counsels, will privately traverse, and publicly oppose, their measures. He will, however, continue in his employment. Instead of suffering any mark of displeasure, he will be distinguished by an unbounded profusion of Court rewards and caresses; because he does what is expected, and all that is expected, from men in office. He helps to keep some form of Administration in being, and keeps it at the same time as weak and divided as possible.

However, we must take care not to be mistaken, or to imagine that such persons have any weight in their opposition. When, by them, Administration is convinced of its insignificancy, they are soon to be convinced of their own. They never are suffered to succeed in their opposition. They and the world are to be satisfied, that neither office, nor authority, nor property, nor ability, eloquence, counsel, skill, or union, are of the least importance; but that the mere influence of the Court, naked of all support, and destitute of all management, is abundantly sufficient for all its own purposes.

When any adverse connexion is to be destroyed, the Cabal seldom appear in the work themselves. They find out some person of whom the party entertains an high opinion. Such a person they endeavour to delude with various pretences. They teach him first to distrust, and then to quarrel with his friends; among whom, by the same arts, they excite a similar diffidence of him; so that in this mutual fear and distrust, he may suffer himself to be employed as the instrument in the change which is brought about. Afterwards they are sure to destroy him in his turn; by setting up in his place some person in whom he had himself reposed the greatest confidence, and who serves to carry off a considerable part of his adherents.

When such a person has broke in this manner with his connexions, he is soon compelled to commit some flagrant act of iniquitous personal hostility against some of them (such as an attempt to strip a particular friend of his family estate),[1] by which the Cabal hope to render the parties utterly irreconcileable. In truth, they have so contrived matters, that people have a greater hatred to the subordinate instruments than to the principal movers.

As in destroying their enemies they make use of instruments not immediately belonging to their corps, so in advancing their own friends they pursue exactly the same method.

---

[1] This refers to the attempt made to deprive the Duke of Portland of his manor and castle of Carlisle, which occasioned the 'Nullum Tempus' bill.

To promote any of them to considerable rank or emolument, they commonly take care that the recommendation shall pass through the hands of the ostensible Ministry: such a recommendation might however appear to the world, as some proof of the credit of Ministers, and some means of increasing their strength. To prevent this, the persons so advanced are directed in all companies, industriously to declare, that they are under no obligations whatsoever to Administration; that they have received their office from another quarter; that they are totally free and independent.

When the Faction has any job of lucre to obtain, or of vengeance to perpetrate, their way is, to select, for the execution, those very persons to whose habits, friendships, principles, and declarations, such proceedings are publicly known to be the most adverse; at once to render the instruments the more odious, and therefore the more dependent, and to prevent the people from ever reposing a confidence in any appearance of private friendship, or public principle.

If the Administration seem now and then, from remissness, or from fear of making themselves disagreeable, to suffer any popular excesses to go unpunished, the Cabal immediately sets up some creature of theirs to raise a clamour against the Ministers, as having shamefully betrayed the dignity of Government. Then they compel the Ministry to become active in conferring rewards and honours on the persons who have been the instruments of their disgrace; and, after having first vilified them with the higher orders for suffering the laws to sleep over the licentiousness of the populace, they drive them (in order to make amends for their former inactivity) to some act of atrocious violence, which renders them completely abhorred by the people. They who remember the riots which attended the Middlesex Election; the opening of the present Parliament; and the transactions relative to Saint George's Fields,[1] will not be at a loss for an application of these remarks.

That this body may be enabled to compass all the ends of its institution, its members are scarcely ever to aim at the high and responsible offices of the State. They are distributed with art and judgement through all the secondary, but efficient, departments of office,

[1] See Lecky, ed. 1892, iii. 319-321, on the riots which then took place. Wilkes was confined in the King's Bench prison, situated in St George's Fields. The mob demanded Wilkes's release, were fired upon by the soldiers, and five men killed.

and through the households of all the branches of the Royal Family: so as on one hand to occupy all the avenues to the Throne; and on the other to forward or frustrate the execution of any measure, according to their own interests. For with the credit and support which they are known to have, though for the greater part in places which are only a genteel excuse for salary, they possess all the influence of the highest posts; and they dictate publicly in almost every thing, even with a parade of superiority. Whenever they dissent (as it often happens) from their nominal leaders, the trained part of the Senate, instinctively in the secret, is sure to follow them; provided the leaders, sensible of their situation, do not of themselves recede in time from their most declared opinions. This latter is generally the case. It will not be conceivable to any one who has not seen it, what pleasure is taken by the Cabal in rendering these heads of office thoroughly contemptible and ridiculous. And when they are become so, they have then the best chance for being well supported.

The members of the Court Faction are fully indemnified for not holding places on the slippery heights of the kingdom, not only by the lead in all affairs, but also by the perfect security in which they enjoy less conspicuous, but very advantageous, situations. Their places are, in express legal tenure, or in effect, all of them for life. Whilst the first and most respectable persons in the kingdom are tossed about like tennis balls, the sport of a blind and insolent caprice, no Minister dares even to cast an oblique glance at the lowest of their body. If an attempt be made upon one of this corps, immediately he flies to sanctuary, and pretends to the most inviolable of all promises. No conveniency of public arrangement is available to remove any one of them from the specific situation he holds; and the slightest attempt upon one of them, by the most powerful Minister, is a certain preliminary to his own destruction.

Conscious of their independence, they bear themselves with a lofty air to the exterior Ministers. Like Janissaries, they derive a kind of freedom from the very condition of their servitude. They may act just as they please; provided they are true to the great ruling principle of their institution. It is, therefore, not at all wonderful, that people should be so desirous of adding themselves to that body, in which they may possess and reconcile satisfactions the most alluring, and seemingly the most contradictory; enjoying at once all the spirited pleasure of independence, and all the gross lucre and fat emoluments of servitude.

Here is a sketch, though a slight one, of the constitution, laws, and policy, of this new Court corporation. The name by which they chuse to distinguish themselves, is that of *King's men*, or the *King's friends*, by an invidious exclusion of the rest of his Majesty's most loyal and affectionate subjects. The whole system, comprehending the exterior and interior Administrations, is commonly called, in the technical language of the Court, *Double Cabinet;* in French or English, as you chuse to pronounce it.

Whether all this be a vision of a distracted brain, or the invention of a malicious heart, or a real Faction in the country, must be judged by the appearances which things have worn for eight years past. Thus far I am certain, that there is not a single public man, in or out of office, who has not, at some time or other, borne testimony to the truth of what I have now related. In particular, no persons have been more strong in their assertions, and louder and more indecent in their complaints, than those who compose all the exterior part of the present Administration; in whose time that Faction has arrived at such an height of power, and of boldness in the use of it, as may, in the end, perhaps bring about its total destruction.

It is true, that about four years ago,[1] during the administration of the Marquis of Rockingham, an attempt was made to carry on Government without their concurrence. However, this was only a transient cloud; they were hid but for a moment; and their constellation blazed out with greater brightness, and a far more vigorous influence, some time after it was blown over. An attempt was at that time made (but without any idea of proscription) to break their corps, to discountenance their doctrines, to revive connexions of a different kind, to restore the principles and policy of the Whigs, to reanimate the cause of Liberty by Ministerial countenance; and then for the first time were men seen attached in office to every principle they had maintained in opposition. No one will doubt, that such men were abhorred and violently opposed by the Court Faction, and that such a system could have but a short duration.

---

[1] Rockingham's first administration only lasted a few months in the winter of 1765-6.

It may appear somewhat affected, that in so much discourse upon this extraordinary Party, I should say so little of the Earl of Bute, who is the supposed head of it. But this was neither owing to affectation nor inadvertence. I have carefully avoided the introduction of personal reflexions of any kind. Much the greater part of the topicks which have been used to blacken this Nobleman, are either unjust or frivolous. At best, they have a tendency to give the resentment of this bitter calamity a wrong direction, and to turn a public grievance into a mean personal, or a dangerous national, quarrel. Where there is a regular scheme of operations carried on, it is a system, and not any individual person who acts in it, that is truly dangerous. This system has not risen solely from the ambition of Lord Bute, but from the circumstances which favoured it, and from an indifference to the constitution which had been for some time growing among our gentry. We should have been tried with it, if the Earl of Bute had never existed; and it will want neither a contriving head nor active members, when the Earl of Bute exists no longer. It is not, therefore, to rail at Lord Bute, but firmly to embody against this Court Party and its practices, which can afford us any prospect of relief in our present condition.

Another motive induces me to put the personal consideration of Lord Bute wholly out of the question. He communicates very little in a direct manner with the greater part of our men of business. This has never been his custom. It is enough for him that he surrounds them with his creatures. Several imagine, therefore, that they have a very good excuse for doing all the work of this Faction, when they have no personal connexion with Lord Bute. But whoever becomes a party to an Administration, composed of insulated individuals, without faith plighted, tie, or common principle; an Administration constitutionally impotent, because supported by no party in the nation; he who contributes to destroy the connexions of men and their trust in one another, or in any sort to throw the dependence of public counsels upon private will and favour, possibly may have nothing to do with the Earl of Bute. It matters little whether he be the friend or the enemy of that particular person. But let him be who or what he will, he abets a Faction that is driving hard to the ruin of his country. He is sapping the foundation of its liberty, disturbing the sources of its domestic tranquillity, weakening its government over its dependencies, degrading it from all its importance in the system of Europe.

It is this unnatural infusion of a *system of Favouritism* into a Government which in a great part of its constitution is popular, that has raised the present ferment in the nation. The people, without entering deeply into its principles, could plainly perceive its effects, in much violence, in a great spirit of innovation, and a general disorder in all the functions of Government. I keep my eye solely on this system; if I speak of those measures which have arisen from it, it will be so far only as they illustrate the general scheme. This is the fountain of all those bitter waters of which, through an hundred different conduits, we have drunk until we are ready to burst. The discretionary power of the Crown in the formation of Ministry, abused by bad or weak men, has given rise to a system, which, without directly violating the letter of any law, operates against the spirit of the whole constitution.

A PLAN of Favouritism for our executory Government is essentially at variance with the plan of our Legislature. One great end undoubtedly of a mixed Government like ours, composed of Monarchy, and of controuls, on the part of the higher people and the lower, is that the Prince shall not be able to violate the laws. This is useful indeed and fundamental. But this, even at first view, is no more than a negative advantage; an armour merely defensive. It is therefore next in order, and equal in importance, *that the discretionary powers which are necessarily vested in the Monarch, whether for the execution of the laws, or for the nomination to magistracy and office, or for conducting the affairs of peace and war, or for ordering the revenue, should all be exercised upon public principles and national grounds, and not on the likings or prejudices, the intrigues or policies, of a Court.* This, I said, is equal in importance to the securing a Government according to law. The laws reach but a very little way. Constitute Government how you please, infinitely the greater part of it must depend upon the exercise of the powers which are left at large to the prudence and uprightness of Ministers of State. Even all the use and potency of the laws depends upon them. Without them, your Commonwealth is no better than a scheme upon paper; and not a living, active, effective constitution. It is possible, that through negligence, or ignorance, or design artfully conducted, Ministers may suffer one part of Government to languish, another to be perverted from its purposes, and every valuable interest of the country to fall into ruin and decay, without possibility of fixing any single act on which a criminal prosecution can be justly grounded. The due arrangement of men in the active part of the State, far from being foreign to the purposes of a wise Government, ought to be among its very first and dearest objects. When, therefore, the abettors of the new system tell us, that between them and their opposers there is nothing but a struggle for power, and that therefore we are no-ways concerned in it; we must tell those who have the impudence to insult us in this manner, that, of all things, we ought to be the most concerned, who and what sort of men they are, that hold the trust of everything that is dear to us. Nothing can render this a point of indifference to the nation, but what must either render us totally desperate, or soothe us into the security of idiots. We must soften into a credulity below the milkiness of infancy, to think all men virtuous. We must be tainted with a malignity truly diabolical, to believe all the world to be equally wicked and corrupt. Men are in public life as in private, some good, some evil. The elevation of the one, and the depression of the other, are the first objects of all true policy. But that form of Government, which, neither in its direct institutions, nor in their immediate tendency, has contrived to throw its affairs into the most trust-worthy hands, but has left its whole executory system to be disposed of agreeably to the uncontrouled pleasure of any one man, however excellent or virtuous, is a plan of polity defective not only in that member, but consequentially erroneous in every part of it.

In arbitrary Governments, the constitution of the Ministry follows the constitution of the Legislature. Both the Law and the Magistrate are the creatures of Will. It must be so. Nothing, indeed, will appear more certain, on any tolerable consideration of this matter, than that *every sort of Government ought to have its Administration correspondent to its Legislature.* If it should be otherwise, things must fall into an hideous disorder. The people of a free Commonwealth, who have taken such care that their laws should be the result of general consent, cannot be so senseless as to suffer their executory system to be composed of persons on whom they have no dependence, and whom no proofs of the public love and confidence have recommended to those powers, upon the use of which the very being of the State depends.

The popular election of magistrates, and popular disposition of rewards and honours, is one of the first advantages of a free State. Without it, or something equivalent to it, perhaps the people cannot long enjoy the substance of freedom; certainly none of the vivifying energy of good Government. The frame of our Commonwealth did not admit of such an actual election: but it provided as well, and (while the spirit of the constitution is preserved) better, for all the effects of it, than by the method of suffrage in any democratic State whatsoever. It had always, until of late, been held the first duty of Parliament, *to refuse to support Government, until power was in the hands of persons who were acceptable to the people, or while factions predominated in the Court in which the nation had no confidence.* Thus all the good effects of popular election were supposed to be secured to us, without the mischiefs attending on perpetual intrigue, and a distinct canvass for every particular office throughout the body of the people. This was the most noble and refined part of our constitution. The people, by their representatives and grandees, were intrusted with a deliberate power in making laws; the King with the controul of his negative. The King was intrusted with the deliberate choice and the election to office; the people had the negative in a Parliamentary refusal to support. Formerly this power of controul was what kept Ministers in awe of Parliaments, and Parliaments in reverence with the people. If the use of this power of controul on the system and persons of Administration is gone, everything is lost, Parliament and all. We may assure ourselves, that if Parliament will tamely see evil men take possession of all the strong-holds of their country, and allow them time and means to fortify themselves, under a pretence of giving them a fair trial, and upon a hope of discovering, whether they will not be reformed by power, and whether their measures will not be better than their morals; such a Parliament will give countenance to their measures also, whatever that Parliament may pretend, and whatever those measures may be.

Every good political institution must have a preventive operation as well as a remedial. It ought to have a natural tendency to exclude bad men from Government, and not to trust for the safety of the State to subsequent punishment alone: punishment, which has ever been tardy and uncertain; and which, when power is suffered in bad hands, may chance to fall rather on the injured than the criminal.

Before men are put forward into the great trusts of the State, they ought by their conduct to have obtained such a degree of estimation in their country, as may be some sort of pledge and security to the publick, that they will not abuse those trusts. It is no mean security for a proper use of power, that a man has shown by the general tenor of his actions, that the affection, the good opinion, the confidence, of his fellow-citizens have been among the principal objects of his life; and that he has owed none of the gradations of his power or fortune to a settled contempt, or occasional forfeiture of their esteem.

That man who before he comes into power has no friends, or who coming into power is obliged to desert his friends, or who losing it has no friends to sympathize with him; he who has no sway among any part of the landed or commercial interest, but whose whole importance has begun with his office, and is sure to end with it; is a person who ought never to be suffered by a controuling Parliament to continue in any of those situations which confer the lead and direction of all our public affairs; because such a man *has no connection with the interest of the people.*

Those knots or cabals of men who have got together, avowedly without any public principle, in order to sell their conjunct iniquity at the higher rate, and are therefore universally odious, ought never to be suffered to domineer in the State; because they have *no connexion with the sentiments and opinions of the people.*

These are considerations which in my opinion enforce the necessity of having some better reason, in a free country, and a free Parliament, for supporting the Ministers of the Crown, than that short one, *That the King has thought proper to appoint them.* There is something very courtly in this. But it is a principle pregnant with all sorts of mischief, in a constitution like ours, to turn the views of active men from the country to the Court. Whatever be the road to power, that is the road which will be trod. If the opinion of the country be of no use as a means of power or consideration, the qualities which usually procure that opinion will be no longer cultivated. And whether it will be right, in a State so popular in its constitution as ours, to leave ambition without popular motives, and to trust all to the operation of pure virtue [1] in the minds of Kings and Ministers, and public men, must be submitted to the judgement and good sense of the people of England.

CUNNING men are here apt to break in, and, without directly controverting the principle, to raise objections from the difficulty under which the Sovereign labours, to distinguish the genuine voice and sentiments of his people, from the clamour of a faction, by which it is so easily counterfeited. The nation, they say, is generally divided into parties, with views and passions utterly irreconcileable. If the King should put his affairs into the hands of any one of them, he is sure to disgust the rest; if he select particular men from among them all, it is an hazard that he disgusts them all. Those who are left out, however divided before, will soon run into a body of opposition; which, being a collection of many discontents into one focus, will without doubt be hot and violent enough. Faction will make its cries resound through the nation, as if

[1] Another allusion to the 'Patriot King.'

the whole were in an uproar, when by far the majority, and much the better part, will seem for awhile as it were annihilated by the quiet in which their virtue and moderation incline them to enjoy the blessings of Government. Besides that, the opinion of the mere vulgar is a miserable rule even with regard to themselves, on account of their violence and instability. So that if you were to gratify them in their humour to-day, that very gratification would be a ground of their dissatisfaction on the next. Now as all these rules of public opinion are to be collected with great difficulty, and to be applied with equal uncertainty as to the effect, what better can a King of England do, than to employ such men as he finds to have views and inclinations most conformable to his own; who are least infected with pride and self-will; and who are least moved by such popular humours as are perpetually traversing his designs, and disturbing his service; trusting that when he means no ill to his people, he will be supported in his appointments, whether he chooses to keep or to change, as his private judgment or his pleasure leads him? He will find a sure resource in the real weight and influence of the Crown, when it is not suffered to become an instrument in the hands of a faction.

I will not pretend to say that there is nothing at all in this mode of reasoning; because I will not assert, that there is no difficulty in the art of Government. Undoubtedly the very best Administration must encounter a great deal of opposition; and the very worst will find more support than it deserves. Sufficient appearances will never be wanting to those who have a mind to deceive themselves. It is a fallacy in constant use with those who would level all things, and confound right with wrong, to insist upon the inconveniences which are attached to every choice, without taking into consideration the different weight and consequence of those inconveniences. The question is not concerning *absolute* discontent or *perfect* satisfaction in Government; neither of which can be pure and unmixed at any time, or upon any system. The controversy is about that degree of good-humour in the people, which may possibly be attained, and ought certainly to be looked for. While some politicians may be waiting to know whether the sense of every individual be against them, accurately distinguishing the vulgar from the better sort, drawing lines between the enterprizes of a faction and the efforts of a people, they may chance to see the Government, which they are so nicely weighing, and dividing, and distinguishing, tumble to the ground in the midst of their wise deliberation. Prudent men, when so great an object as the security of Government, or even its peace, is at stake, will not run risque of a decision which may be fatal to it. They who can read the political sky will see an hurricane in a cloud no bigger than an hand at the very edge of the horizon, and will run into the first harbour. No lines can be laid down for civil or political wisdom. They are a matter incapable of exact definition. But, though no man can draw a stroke between the confines of day and night, yet light and darkness are upon the whole tolerably distinguishable. Nor will it be impossible for a Prince to find out such a mode of Government, and such persons to administer it, as will give a great degree of content to his people; without any curious and anxious research for that abstract, universal, perfect harmony, which while he is seeking, he abandons those means of ordinary tranquillity which are in his power without any research at all.

It is not more the duty than it is the interest of a Prince, to aim at giving tranquillity to his Government. But those who advise him may have an interest in disorder and confusion. If the opinion of the people is against them, they will naturally wish that it should have no prevalence. Here it is that the people must on their part show themselves sensible of their own value. Their whole importance, in the first instance, and afterwards their whole freedom, is at stake. Their freedom cannot long survive their importance. Here it is that the natural strength of the kingdom, the great peers, the leading landed gentlemen, the opulent merchants and manufacturers, the substantial yeomanry, must interpose, to rescue their Prince, themselves, and their posterity.

We are at present at issue upon this point. We are in the great crisis of this contention; and the part which men take, one way or other, will serve to discriminate their characters and their principles. Until the matter is decided, the country will remain in its present confusion. For while a system of Administration is attempted, entirely repugnant to the genius of the people, and not conformable to the plan of their Government, everything must necessarily be disordered for a time, until this system destroys the constitution, or the constitution gets the better of this system.

XIII

BURKE'S THIRD LETTER ON A REGICIDE PEACE

[This the last work from Burke's pen was written exactly a century ago, between January and Burke's death on 9 July 1797; it has on the one hand been held to exceed in intellectual magnitude all other single efforts of the human brain, while on the other a great living critic has described these letters as 'deplorable.'[1] But there is no difference of opinion as to their literary qualities, and the passage reprinted here, with which the third letter closes, is the most splendid peroration in the English language. The letter was written on the failure of Lord Malmesbury's peace mission to the French Directorate in the autumn of 1796, but was not published till after Burke's death.]

IF then the real state of this nation is such as I have described, and I am only apprehensive that you may think I have taken too much pains to exclude all doubt on this question—if no class is lessened in it's numbers, or in it's stock, or in it's conveniencies, or even it's

[1] Morley, *Burke*, ed. 1888, p. 293.

luxuries; if they build as many habitations, and as elegant and as commodious as ever, and furnish them with every chargeable decoration, and every prodigality of ingenious invention, that can be thought of by those who even encumber their necessities with superfluous accommodation; if they are as numerously attended; if their equipages are as splendid; if they regale at table with as much or more variety of plenty than ever; if they are clad in as expensive and changeful a diversity according to their tastes and modes; if they are not deterred from the pleasures of the field by the charges, which Government has wisely turned from the culture to the sports of the field; if the theatres are as rich and as well filled, and greater, and at a higher price than ever; and, what is more important than all, if it is plain from the treasures which are spread over the soil, or confided to the winds, and the seas, that there are as many who are indulgent to their propensities of parsimony, as others to their voluptuous desires, and that the pecuniary capital grows instead of diminishing; on what ground are we authorized to say that a nation gambolling in an ocean of superfluity is undone by want? With what face can we pretend, that they who have not denied any one gratification to any one appetite, have a right to plead poverty in order to famish their virtues, and to put their duties on short allowance? That they are to take the law from an imperious enemy, and can contribute no longer to the honour of their king, to the support of the independence of their country, to the salvation of that Europe, which, if it falls, must crash them with its gigantick ruins? How can they affect to sweat, and stagger, and groan under their burdens, to whom the mines of Newfoundland, richer than those of Mexico and Peru, are now thrown in as a make-weight in the scale of their exorbitant opulence? What excuse can they have to faint, and creep, and cringe, and prostrate themselves at the footstool of ambition and crime, who, during a short though violent struggle, which they have never supported with the energy of men, have amassed more to their annual accumulation, than all the well-husbanded capital that enabled their ancestors by long, and doubtful, and obstinate conflicts to defend, and liberate, and vindicate the civilized world? But I do not accuse the People of England. As to the great majority of the nation, they have done whatever in their several ranks, and conditions, and descriptions, was required of them by their relative situations in society; and from those the great mass of mankind cannot depart, without the subversion of all publick order. They look up to that Government, which they obey that they may be protected. They ask to be led and directed by those rulers, whom Providence and the laws of their country have set over them, and under their guidance to walk in the ways of safety and honour. They have again delegated the greatest trust which they have to bestow to those faithful representatives who made their true voice heard against the disturbers and destroyers of Europe. They suffered, with unapproving acquiescence, solicitations, which they had in no shape desired, to an unjust and usurping Power, whom they had never provoked, and whose hostile menaces they did not dread. When the exigencies of the publick service could only be met by their voluntary zeal, they started forth with an ardour which outstripped the wishes of those, who had injured them by doubting, whether it might not be necessary to have recourse to compulsion. They have, in all things, reposed an enduring, but not an unreflecting confidence.

That confidence demands a full return; and fixes a responsibility on the Ministers entire and undivided. The People stands acquitted; if the war is not carried on in a manner suited to it's objects. If the publick honour is tarnished; if the public safety suffers any detriment; they, not the People, are to answer it, and they alone. It's armies, it's navies, are given to them without stint or restriction. It's treasures are poured out at their feet. It's constancy is ready to second all their efforts. They are not to fear a responsibility for acts of manly adventure. The responsibility which they are to dread, is, lest they should shew themselves unequal to the expectation of a brave people. The more doubtful may be the constitutional and œconomical questions, upon which they have received so marked a support, the more loudly they are called upon to support this great war, for the success of which their country is willing to supersede considerations of no slight importance. Where I speak of responsibility, I do not mean to exclude that species of it, which the legal powers of the country have a right finally to exact from those who abuse a public trust; but high as this is, there is a responsibility which attaches on them, from which the whole legitimate power of the kingdom cannot absolve them; there is a responsibility to conscience and to glory; a responsibility to the existing world, and to that posterity, which men of their eminence cannot avoid for glory or for shame; a responsibility to a tribunal, at which, not only Ministers, but Kings and Parliaments, but even Nations themselves, must one day answer.

www.ingramcontent.com/pod-product-compliance
Lightning Source LLC
Chambersburg PA
CBHW031852220426
43663CB00006B/597